OSPREY COMBAT A

RA-5C VIGILANTE UNITS IN COMBAT

14931
USS RAN

SERIES EDITOR: TONY HOLMES

OSPREY COMBAT AIRCRAFT • 51

RA-5C VIGILANTE UNITS IN COMBAT

ROBERT R 'BOOM' POWELL

OSPREY
PUBLISHING

First published in Great Britain in 2004 by Osprey Publishing,
Midland House, West Way, Botley, Oxford OX2 0PH, UK
44-02 23rd St, Suite 219, Long Island City, NY 11101, USA
Email: info@ospreypublishing.com

Transferred to digital print on demand 2010

First published 2004
3rd impression 2007

Printed and bound in Great Britain

A CIP catalogue record for this book is available from the British Library

ISBN: 978 1 84176 749 9

Edited by Tony Holmes
Page design by Tony Truscott
Cover Artwork by Mark Postlethwaite
Aircraft Profiles by Jim Laurier
Scale Drawings by Mark Styling
Index by Alan Thatcher
Origination by PPS Grasmere Ltd., Leeds, UK
Typeset in Adobe Garamond, Rockwell and Univers

Editor's note
To make this best-selling series as authoritative as possible, the editor would be extremely interested in hearing from any individual who may have relevant photographs, documentation or first-hand experiences relating to the elite pilots, and their aircraft, of the various theatres of war. Any material used will be fully credited to its original source. Please contact Tony Holmes at 16 Sandilands, Chipstead, Sevenoaks, Kent, TN13 2SP or via email at tony.holmes@zen.co.uk

The Woodland Trust
Osprey Publishing is supporting the Woodland Trust, the UK's leading woodland conservation charity, by funding the dedication of trees.

www.ospreypublishing.com

Front cover
On 1 March 1971, Lt Cdr Barry Gastrock and Lt Emy Conrad, crewing an RA-5C Vigilante of RVAH-6, took a remarkable photograph by accident while performing a reconnaissance mission over North Vietnam from USS *Kitty Hawk* (CVA-63). Their planned route crossed over itself so as to allow the crew to get comprehensive photographic coverage of the Song Ca River. This area was well inside the SAM envelopes around the city of Vinh. Heading south, the Vigilante appeared back over the river juncture at Hung Nghia less than four minutes after crossing the same village in a westerly direction. AAA had been sporadic on the jet's first pass over the area, and there had been no missile warnings when Lt Conrad saw a flash in his viewfinder, heard a 'whumpf' and was thrown against his seat-straps. The coast was not far away, and the crew soon went 'feet wet' and subsequently carried out a routine landing back aboard *Kitty Hawk*.

A short while later in the ship's intelligence centre, a photo-interpreter cranked the six inch-wide film from one massive spool to another across the light-table and stopped in surprise. Perfectly framed by the Vigilante's vertical camera was an SA-2 surface-air-missile (SAM) still under boost. The crew was called in to see the near miss. Since there was no terrain visible in the frame, they assumed the SAM passed beside the RA-5C as Lt Cdr Gastrock banked hard to head for home. Knowing the focal length of the camera and the size of an SA-2, the photogrammeters computed that the missile had passed just 104 ft away from the Vigilante's belly. No one knows why it did not detonate. (*Cover artwork by Mark Postlethwaite*)

CONTENTS

PREFACE – BDA RUN

The dust, dirt and debris from 100 Mk 82 500-lb bombs was still settling back to the ground as the Vigilante began its photo run. The pilot had both afterburners blazing, and he lowered the nose of his aircraft to pick up more speed. In the back cockpit, the Reconnaissance Attack Navigator (RAN) checked that the film counters were running down, the image-motion bars were tracking and the inertial navigation readouts were correct, all while watching the ALQ scope for any signs of SAM radar lock-ons and missile launches. The Vigilante was doing 650 mph as the wings snapped level over the primary target. Inside the planned turn, the Phantom II escort was in full afterburner trying to keep up.

The Vietnamese gunners who had not been injured in the attack had reloaded their weapons as fast as they could, and they began to shoot as the RA-5C came over the target. The smaller guns tracked the fast moving aircraft while an 87 mm site put up a barrage of exploding shells where they hoped the Vigilante would be.

The pilot jinked left to throw off the track of the gunners, avoid the shell bursts and get closer to one of the SAM sites which had been attacked. Tracers streaked the air, the ALQ screen was a mass of pulsing golden strobes and missile lock warnings warbled in the crew's earphones. The RAN continued to monitor the reconnaissance and navigation systems as the aeroplane swerved and bounced. The Radar Intercept Officer (RIO) in the escorting Phantom II called out gunfire when he saw it.

After long, breathless minutes, the two aeroplanes cleared the target area. The RAN moved a cursor handle, punched a button and told his pilot to 'Follow steering'. On the pilot's instrument panel a needle swung towards the southeast, and numbers showing the distance to their aircraft carrier spun up. They were still 40 miles from the safety of the Tonkin Gulf, and remained in afterburner until off the coast, and having reported 'Feet Wet' to the carrier.

Such was a typical BDA (Bomb Damage Assessment) mission flown by RVAH squadrons during the whole of the air war in Vietnam.

The vast majority of RA-5C flights were either BDA or route reconnaissance. The Vigilante had the most sophisticated suite of reconnaissance systems of any aircraft flying at the time. It also had the highest loss rate of any carrier-based aircraft during the war in South-East Asia.

The Vigilante crews used to taunt the attack and fighter pilots;

'We have to get back from our missions to be successful. Once you hot-shots have dropped your bombs, you're done. Furthermore, it is our photos that are firm evidence that a target has been destroyed so you don't have to go back. Our cameras don't lie.'

'Unarmed and Unafraid' was the cynical motto of the Vigilante photo-reconnaissance crews who flew into the world's most heavily defended airspace.

Robert R 'Boom' Powell
Virginia Beach, Virginia
July 2004

LINEAGE

The North American Aviation (NAA) RA-5C Vigilante had its origins in the US Navy's heavy attack aircraft programme. Early atomic bombs weighed thousands of pounds, and required a large aeroplane to drop them. This was not a problem for the land-based US Air Force, which operated from bases that boasted long concrete runways, but getting an A-bomb off a ship was a different matter entirely.

First, the Navy toyed with the idea of using P2V Neptunes launched off carriers with supplemental rockets. Although the Neptune had tremendous range, it was a slow, reciprocating engine aeroplane and much too large to recover on board ship. Furthermore, with any more than two P2Vs on deck, no other flying was possible. The concept was tested, but was never anything more than a stop-gap measure.

Next, NAA designed and built the AJ Savage to meet the requirements for an atomic bomb-carrying aeroplane capable of flying off and then recovering back aboard a carrier at sea. The Savage was the world's first heavy, multi-engined carrier aircraft. However, it was powered by two reciprocating engines and was slow, even with a supplemental jet engine fitted in the fuselage. Eventually, the Savage became a tanker for the new practice of aerial refuelling, and saw further service for a few more years.

Douglas Aircraft came up with a winner in the A3D Skywarrior. Soon known as the 'Whale', it was effective at delivering heavy bomb loads, conventional or nuclear – in the early days an engine pod would occasionally rip off during the pull-up into a loft manoeuvre, resulting in the bomb landing way short of the intended target, and an unexpected and rapid roll. The Skywarrior was fast – the fastest Navy aeroplane built without an afterburner – but it was subsonic. Supersonic was the requirement of the time, so NAA developed the Mach 2 Vigilante.

After the Navy deleted the aircraft strategic nuclear mission, which also affected the A-5, the A-3 was put into roles such as a dedicated air-refuelling tanker and an electronics warfare platform, which gave it a

The North American AJ Savage bomber had two reciprocating engines and a jet in the tail. Savages were operational during the Navy's changeover from the all-blue to grey and white paint scheme (*Backstall*)

The Douglas A3D Skywarrior was the Vigilante's predecessor in carrier-based heavy attack squadrons. The black and white checked band that gave VAH-11 its nickname 'Checkertails' and the old squadron insignia are visible on both jets seen in this photograph (*Backstall*)

service life longer than its Vigilante replacement as a dedicated bomber. The 'Whale' remains the only challenger to the Vigilante for the title of the largest aircraft to routinely operate off a carrier. If the contest is made the largest and fastest, then the Vigilante wins. The Skywarrior could launch at a heavier weight (its trap weight was the same), and had a wider wingspan, (the Vigilante was slightly longer), but the A-5 was faster, whether measuring approach or top speed.

Designed as a high-flying, high-speed strategic nuclear bomber, the A-5 may have introduced more new technological features than any other aircraft in history, including:

- variable engine-throat inlets with profile and area adjustments for flight at high Mach numbers.
- lightweight, high strength wing skins manufactured by milling a single piece of aluminum-lithium alloy.
- ducted engine bleed-air blown over flight surfaces for improved lift and control at low airspeeds.
- major structures and frames were built out of Titanium.
- first variable inlet using horizontal ramp geometry.
- a fully retractable refuelling probe in the forward fuselage.
- the first production fly-by-wire control system.
- a single-piece, bird-proof, Mach 2 capable windscreen made of stretched acrylic.
- gold-plating in the engine bays to reflect heat.
- first monopulse radar with terrain avoidance features.
- first operational heads-up display (HUD).
- first Weapons-Navigation System with inertial auto-navigation coupled to radar and television (ASB-12).
- airborne digital computer for weapon and navigation computations(VERDAN).
- fully integrated auto pilot/air data system.

The Vigilante also had no conventional flight controls. The A-5 did not have ailerons, elevators or a rudder. Spoilers provided roll control and acted as speed brakes. The horizontal tail surfaces were solid slabs. Together, they controlled pitch, and were adjusted separately for roll trim. The vertical tail was also one piece, rather than a hinged rudder. Each of these gave the RA-5C some handling quirks.

Like all jets the Vigilante had a yaw augmentation system. When you taxied behind another Vigilante, the vertical slab would move in response to the rudder pedals, which were used for nose wheel steering while the 'Yaw Aug' responded to spurious inputs by shaking and shimmying the tail like a dog trying to get dry!

Landing Signal Officers (LSOs), while waving the Vigilante on board the carrier, could see every tiny movement of the horizontal slab because it was so big. A well flown Vigilante pass had the nose steady on speed while the slabs fluttered and twitched from the pilot's small, constant stick inputs.

This photograph was released by NAA when it was touting the A-5's conventional weapons capabilities following problems with the jet's complex nuclear bomb delivery system. This particular aircraft is probably a rare A-5B. While a full series of ordnance tests were conducted, during which the Vigilante proved itself to be a stable and effective weapons platform, the A-5 never shot a rocket or dropped a bomb in anger (*EBAL*)

Neither of these was apparent in the cockpit while flying, but using the spoilers to roll certainly was. Rather than the centre of the roll axis being through the pilot's belly, as it is on most aeroplanes, it felt like it was out on the high wing. Jam the control stick to the side, and one seemed to drop as the roll started.

The first flight of an A3J (as the aircraft was initially designated) took place in August 1958. While still in the development stage, Vigilantes set several speed and altitude records. One such flight took place in December 1960, when an A3J set an altitude/load record by carrying a 1000-kg (2400-lb) payload on a zoom-profile flight that peaked at 91,451 ft.

Improvements (especially in its fuel capacity) were made with the advent of the A3J-2/A5B in the early 1960s. Only two A5Bs were delivered to the Navy before two events complicated identification of the Vigilante. First, NAA merged with the Rockwell Corporation to become North American Rockwell (NAR). Second, the Department of Defense redesignated all aircraft to a unified system. The A3J became the A-5.

In June 1961, the first Vigilantes went to VAH-3 at NAS Sanford, Florida, to train crews and maintenance personnel. 'Heavy Three' had been the RAG (Replacement Air Group training unit) for the A3D, so the transition was a natural – all A-3 training was subsequently performed by VAH-123 at NAS Whidbey Island, in Washington state. The men in the back cockpits of the A-5s were BNs (Bombardier-Navigators), and many were enlisted men until, in 1962, the Navy decreed that there would be no more enlisted BNs, and many former chiefs and petty officers rapidly became ensigns.

VAH-3 flew two A3Js marked with flamboyant orange trim, these jets being used for experimental work at the Naval Weapons Facility. This publicity photograph with local beauty pageant contestants was taken in 1962 in Sanford, Florida (*Backstall*)

As A3J-1s were delivered from NAR in Columbus, Ohio, two more squadrons transitioned from the A3D – VAH-1 'Smoking Tigers' and VAH-7 'Peacemakers'.

The latter unit became the first squadron to deploy with the Vigilante when it took a dozen A3Js on board USS *Enterprise* (CVAN-65) for the ship and aircraft's first extended time at sea in early August 1962. The carrier's planned stay in the Mediterranean was cut short, however, when the Cuban Missile

Crisis arose in October 1962. VAH-7 left the carrier and was placed on standby status at NAS Sanford, but the unit did not fly any missions directly related to Cuba. CVAN-65's Mediterranean deployment finally resumed in early February 1963, and lasted for seven months. In August 1963 VAH-1 went to sea in USS *Independence* (CVA-62) with 12 A-5A (the redesignation now in effect) supersonic bombers.

VAH-7 deployed again on *Enterprise* in February 1964, and it had been in the Mediterranean for five months when the carrier was joined by the cruiser USS *Long Beach* (CGN-9) and the destroyer USS *Bainbridge* (DLGN-25) to form a nuclear-powered task force for an around-the-world cruise. Operation *Sea Orbit* ended in October 1964.

Wearing full-pressure suits for high altitude flight, three A3J crews of VAH-7 walk to their jets across the flight deck of the brand new nuclear-powered aircraft carrier USS *Enterprise* (CVAN-65). The suits were not popular as they were difficult to don and uncomfortable anywhere besides sitting in the cockpit. They did keep you alive if cockpit pressurisation failed above 50,000 ft, however (*Backstall*)

RECONNAISSANCE BIRD

After much high-level political wrangling and bitter inter-service arguments, the US Navy gave up its aircraft delivery strategic nuclear bombardment role in 1963. The Vigilante suddenly had no mission.

Work on the reconnaissance version of the aircraft, designated the RA-5C, had begun while VAH-7 and VAH-1 were on the only

Left
An unpainted RA-5C used to train the type's first batch of flight crews flies over the North American plant in Columbus, Ohio, where it was built in 1963. Dave Turner wrote of the six weeks of training, 'We took the aircraft from the Navy rep at the factory before they were painted, and before Pax River flew or had them for carrier trials. We called the paint job "Shit Brindle Brown"' (*Turner*)

Right
Photographers Mates using a winch to load a camera module into Sensor Station 4, which could house a variety of camera configurations

Early RA-5C crewmen (both air and ground) pose at NAA's Columbus plant. They are, standing, from left to right, Lt(jg) D A Turner, Lt J M Morgan, PHC M B Massie, Lt Cdrs C J Youngblade and J W Ollson, Lts N Pruden, C B Moore and G L Coffee and Lt Cdr C E Thompson. Kneeling (from left to right) are ADJ (jet mechs) T E Phillips, R E Sprague, W W Hamilton, J L Patterson and C J Beaulieu. The NAS Sanford base newspaper the *Sandfly* published the following article about these men on 8 November 1963;

'During the months of August and September, selected flight crews from Heavy Attack Squadrons Three and Five underwent extensive training in the Navy's newest reconnaissance attack aircraft, the RA-5C. Their training programme was conducted at the NAA plant at Columbus, Ohio, and kept the crews busy for five-and-a-half full weeks. The training emphasised the reconnaissance aspects of the new system, and each crew logged some 30 hours while wringing out the multiple systems of the aircraft. All flight crews were initiated into NAA's exclusive "Sod Dodger" club when they logged night time flying at low level utilising the Terrain Avoidance System. The two VAH-3 crews will form the nucleus for the reconnaissance training within HATWING ONE's training squadron, and the two VAH-5 crews are the first to receive training prior to their squadron receiving the RA-5C in the very near future' (*Turner*)

deployments of the A3J/A-5A. The Cuban Missile Crisis gave added impetus to the development of the reconnaissance version. The A-5B was converted into a reconnaissance machine through the addition of a belly 'canoe' containing interchangeable sensors and side-looking radar. The RA-5C prototype was first flown in June 1962, and a total of 43 new airframes were built. All 18 surviving B-models, as well as 43 A-models, were converted to RA-5C specification by NAR in its Columbus, Ohio, factory.The first completed jet went to VAH-3, which began training the reconnaissance mission, as well as continuing training for the attack role.

The RA-5C was the airborne portion of a total reconnaissance system, with the Integrated Operational Intelligence Center (IOIC) being the ground or ship-based part.

The earliest aerial photography was done with bulky cameras taking individual images on heavy plates. Later, automatic cameras took a series of photographs on rolls of film. An apparent three-dimensional effect was achieved by viewing overlapping images through a stereo lens, and this provided a major improvement in photo interpretation. Although time and altitude were imprinted on each frame, working out where the picture was taken still depended on the pilot's navigation log and a mission trace from the slow-firing forward oblique camera. When the photo-aircraft returned, the film was developed one roll at a time and studied on a light table.

The RA-5C/IOIC system was a vast improvement. The key element was the Vigilante's ASB-12 Inertial Navigation System (INS), which printed a small data-matrix block in the corner of each photo frame, and at regular intervals on the continuous side-looking radar (SLR) and infra-red (IR) imagery. This block showed the aircraft position, as well as time and altitude. The machine which developed the film was originally classified confidential, but similar machines can today be found in every local One Hour Photo shop. The rapidly processed film was then mounted on a viewing machine, which read the data-matrix block and correlated to geographic locations while giving stereo images and side by side comparison with other cameras, IR maps or SLR imagery. The tape on which the Passive Electronic Counter Measures (PECM) recorded its radar locating information was read on the same viewer.

Each RVAH squadron had four Air Intelligence Officers (AIO), one of whom was a PECM specialist, a photo officer and several Photo Interpreters (PIs), Photo Technicians (PTs) and Photo Mate (PM) ratings assigned to work with the mass of data.

THE 'ELEPHANT'

The Vigilante soon earned the sobriquet of the Elephant. The length of the nose and the way it stuck far out in front of the nose-wheel was part of the image, but more than that was the sound its General Electric J79-GE-10 turbojet engines buried deep in the long, square intakes made when taxiing and on landing approach. Some wit described the pulsing, loud moan as the mating call of a female elephant. The name stuck, and two or more A-5s moving on the flight deck preparing to catapult was called the 'dance of the elephants'.

Over the years, 'Elephant' was used less and less for the aircraft, and with its official name, Vigilante, not being the easiest word to say, this was usually shortened to 'Vige' or 'Vigi'. 'Vige' has one syllable and rhymes with ridge, while 'Vigi' is spoken with two syllables. Because of its size, reconnaissance was also usually abbreviated to 'recce' or 'recon'.

The other way to get a Vigilante aboard ship – an A3J is hoisted on to the lowered deck-edge elevator of an unidentified carrier. Both wings and tail are folded in order to squeeze the big jet into the hangar bay (*EBAL*)

THE MEN IN BACK

The RANs who rode in the back cockpit of the Vigilante were a special breed. Earning designation as a qualified Reconnaissance Attack Navigator required intelligence, perseverance, dexterity, multiple skills and excellent aeronautical adaptation. Only the best made it.

F-4 Phantom IIs had their RIOs, A-6 Intruders their bombardier-navigators (BNs) and the 'Q-birds' (EA-3, EA-6, EA-1) their electronic counter-countermeasures officers. Vigilantes had RANs. All were mission specialised terms within the larger category of Naval Flight Officer, (NFO). Like pilots, they

went through a standard syllabus in basic training, with a degree of specialisation in advanced training. Final assignment was given with a nod to individual preference, but dependent on class standing. At one time, newly designated NFOs on their way to reconnaissance were sent to a 'good deal' photography school in Pensacola, Florida. Here, they were provided with cameras and unlimited rolls of film and sent out to find subjects and hone their skills. The young women on the sandy Gulf beaches were a favourite target!

The 'Recce RAG' was a demanding combination of flying and ground school. First flights were made in a TA-3B 'Whale' fitted with extra seats and radar scopes in what had been the aircraft's bomb-bay. The ex-bomber's weapons/navigation system was the ASB-1, which was a predecessor of the ASB-12 carried in the A-5.

Usually, NFOs and pilots were paired up for the entire syllabus, and if the composition of the class allowed, new NFOs were matched with experienced pilots, and vice versa. Some of the best tactical crews in the fleet had started in RVAH-3 together.

Unlike attack or fighter aircraft training, where crews learned to fly in sections with other jets, most RA-5C missions were flown alone. There was an immediate debrief after the training mission, but the final grades

The A3J initially had two wing stations, but NAA strengthened the wing structure on the A3J-2/A-5B model so that four stores struts could be installed to carry weapons or fuel tanks. In the frontline, these stations were most frequently used to carry a small pod that dispensed 5-lb practice bombs, or as the attachment point for the cameras' flasher pod. The huge 400-gallon drop tanks seen in this photograph were intended to give the Vigilante more range in its strategic role. Even the RVAH squadrons were required to carry them for contingency operations. Because of the tanks' weight and drag, less than a quarter of the fuel they housed added to the jet's range, the rest being burned while carrying the tanks themselves. These stores were never carried operationally (*EBAL*)

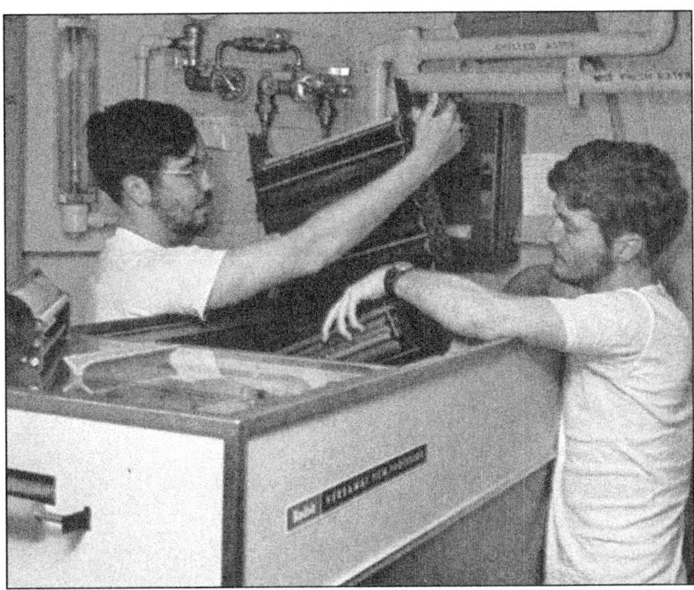

Technicians work on the computer that was at the heart of the IOIC

A view of the pilot's instrument panel while the RA-5C cruises over Vietnam at 19,000 ft. Once the Heads-Up-Display was removed (it sat where the steel bar is), the Vigilante offered the pilot the most unobstructed view of any aeroplane then in Navy service. In a prominent position at the top centre is the G-meter. The aircraft required an overstress inspection at 4 Gs, which all pilots tried to avoid. New pilots going through the RAG would be asked what the knob (to the left in the picture) with 'Push for Release' on it was for, and dared to try it in flight. The answer was nothing at all, as these activated the jet's nuclear blast shields, which had been removed following the Vigilante's abandonment of the bomber mission (*Powell*)

were determined the next day after the film had been processed and reviewed – it is difficult to argue with a photo. Final syllabus flights were to the ship for carrier landings.

Most of the initial cadre when the Vigilante was new came from A-3s, and even AJ Savages, where they had been BNs. The broader category in those days was NAO for Naval Aviation Officer or Observer – the observer role traces its lineage back to the Royal Flying Corps in World War 1. Many BNs were enlisted men who came into the cockpit by first being mechanics or technicians.

Colin Pemberton is a good example. He enlisted in the Navy and became an AMH (Aviation Mechanic, Hydraulics), and as a 2nd Class Petty Officer was a BN in Savages. 'Pem' deployed with VC-7 (later redesignated VAH-7, then RVAH-7) for what became an 11-month sojourn in the Western Pacific because of the Quemoy-Matsu Crisis.

Back in Sanford, he transitioned to A3Ds, and became an instructor in advanced weapons delivery. Pemberton became a Chief Petty Officer and was in the first class for the A3J Vigilante at VAH-3. In 1962 he reported to VAH-1 and went to sea on *Independence*. Although the jet was not yet certified for it, he was with pilot Lt Cdr Jim Bell for the first ever Vigilante barricade engagement. Months later, back in Sanford, they had a complete hydraulic failure and had to eject. The rocket-ride made Pemberton one of the very few enlisted men to have ejected. They were also the first crew to survive an ejection from a Vigilante.

When it came to maintaining the jet's myriad systems, groundcrews could gain intimate access to the Vigilante's inner workings, as this photograph clearly shows. The nose radome went up electrically and the radar antenna, processing unit and 'ball', which housed the inertial-sensing unit, swung down on a shelf (*EBAL*)

Soon after came the decree 'No enlisted BNs', and so those who were eligible applied for the Limited Duty Officer programme (LDO). Pemberton, and a good percentage of the other 118 enlisted B/Ns become LDO/NFOs. Surviving two combat cruises in RA-5Cs, he retired as a lieutenant commander after 30 years in the Navy.

BN continued to be the term for the men in the back of the A3J (later the A-5A). When the mission changed with the arrival of the RA-5C, an R for reconnaissance was added, and even after the attack role was abandoned, the A remained, hence RAN.

The RAN was at the heart of the reconnaissance mission. His job was to run the ASB-12 inertial navigation system (INS) which integrated a radar and television (the television scanner lens was in the small glass blister on the bottom of the Vigilante's nose) for updating the navigation and target detection. All the pilot had in the front cockpit was a steering bar and distance readout. The most frequent command from the back seat was, 'Follow steering'.

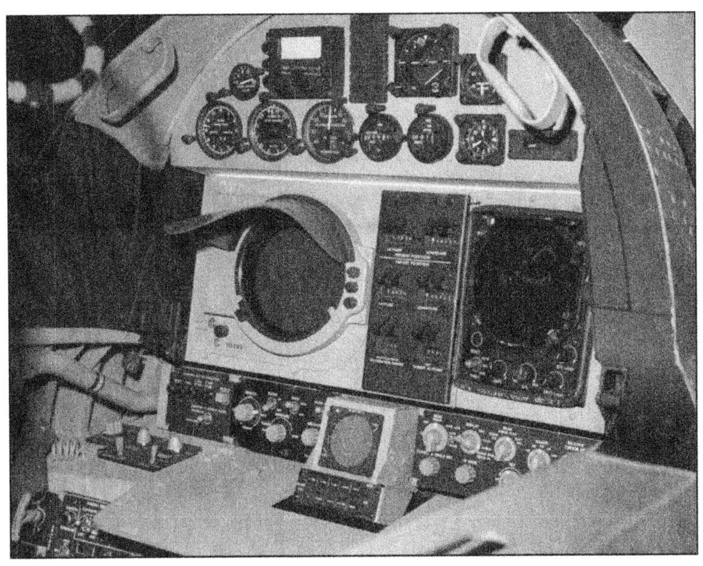

The centre console of the RAN's cockpit. The round screen with the hood displayed either radar or television imagery, while the small square unit at the top of the console was the optical viewfinder, with the navigation readouts in between. Flight instruments were above the hooded display, and the amber radar homing and warning (RHAW) scope was in the middle of the hinged work table (*Conrad*)

Additionally, the RAN had the controls for a suite of sophisticated cameras. No matter how much the Vigilante was manoeuvring, during a photo run, he had to monitor film usage, exposure settings and, most importantly, the Image Motion Compensation (IMC). The optical viewfinder had an opening in the belly of the jet, and through a series of lens, it gave the RAN a look at the ground superimposed with moving lines of light. His job was to adjust the lines to match the aircraft's speed over the ground. Add the controls for an IR mapping unit, SLR and various ECMs, plus normal crew coordination, and his duties kept the RAN busier than a bartender at last call.

The back cockpit had only two small windows mounted high up – leftovers from the Vigilante's origins as a nuclear bomber. There were interior panels that slid over them to shut out all light. Pilots used to accuse the RANs of not being able to see anything, and the navigator would retort that he could see more, not less. The radar reached out 200 miles, the TV as far as air clarity would permit, and he could see the ground beneath the jet from the forward horizon to past the vertical. Could the pilot see what was directly below, or look at the landing gear?

The television system did have a peculiarity – the farther from straight ahead the lens was pointed, the farther it was tilted. On a run using the oblique (pointed to the side) cameras, the TV would be pointed to one side to check distance from the target and the apparent horizon would be at 45 degrees. When checking that the landing gear was 'down' by looking aft, the wheels would be sticking 'up'!

Because of where the TV lens was located, the RAN saw the meatball at the ship lower than the pilot. When only slightly low on glidepath, the backseater would be looking at a red, flashing ball. Remaining quiet took steady nerves. LSOs claimed that the method some RA-5C pilots used to land was to have the RAN look in the viewfinder and call, 'Water, water, steel', so they would know when to make a play for the deck.

The first fleet squadron to receive the RA-5C was RVAH-5, its change in designation arriving almost simultaneously with the first of the modified Vigilantes. After training and work-ups, RVAH-5 deployed in USS *Ranger* (CVA-61) to the Pacific on 5 August 1964. Just days later North Vietnamese torpedo-boats attacked US Navy ships. *Ranger* sped to the Tonkin Gulf, and the combat career of the RA-5C Vigilante began.

The small locking tabs are out while the radome is raised, exposing the radar antenna. The stainless steel probe was an airspeed sensor as well as the 'shock-wave splitter' for supersonic flight (*Smith*)

COMBAT DEVELOPMENT

The first 18 months of the conflict in South-east Asia were difficult for RVAH-5, the reconnaissance community in general and US Navy carrier aviation. A war that had been a smouldering, internal struggle was now drawing the United States in deeper and deeper as it moved into a new phase. Action in South Vietnam continued much as before, but over North Vietnam, American warplanes began a campaign to win a war using air power alone.

The first RA-5C squadron to deploy to the conflict, RVAH-5 entered combat with a jet and a complicated reconnaissance system that were both brand new. The Navy had instituted a programme of contractor support for the new complex aircraft types then coming into the fleet, and the A-6 Intruder, F-4 Phantom II and RA-5C Vigilante all had teams from the manufacturers assisting and advising the sailors in maintaining what were no longer 'aeroplanes', but 'weapons systems'.

Besides having a new aeroplane, the reconnaissance community, under the supervision of Commander of Reconnaissance Wing One (CRAW-1, which controlled all RA-5C units when ashore), had to learn how to

With the Golden Gate bridge in the background, *Ranger* departs San Francisco on 5 August 1964 en route to Hawaii and the South China Sea. All three of the Vigilantes visible in this photograph were from the batch of A-5Bs converted to RA-5C standard. Confined to operations over South Vietnam on this cruise, RVAH-5 was kept busy providing photo intelligence to allow the Navy to plan future attack routes (*Mersky*)

integrate their squadrons with ships' IOIC. There were new systems to supplement traditional photography, such as SLR and the sophisticated, and fragile, PECM. Air reconnaissance tactics from previous wars also had to be re-examined and evaluated against the current situation.

On the carriers going to war, the commanders had to adjust to the latest threat and the latest rules. Some tactics were proved sound, others ineffective to fatal. Air wing commanders, captains of the ships and embarked admirals and their staffs all had to find out what worked best in the first months of the air war in Vietnam. Despite contradictory and politically driven directives from Washington, able officers got the job done.

An SLR image of the coast of North Vietnam. The dark stripe on the right was directly under the RA-5C. The print was made from a section of a continuous roll of film. Photo interpreters added the arrows and notes to the negative (WBLCs were 'Water Borne Logistics Craft') (*Conrad*)

Most Navy squadrons were mated to an air wing that embarked on a particular carrier again and again. This system provided continuity and an experienced team from year to year. The RVAH squadrons of CRAW-1 were deployed differently, however. Since they were all at a single shore base, there was no West Coast-East Coast division like fighter and attack squadrons had. The same Vigilante squadron being assigned to the same air wing and ship for two deployments in a row was rare. What was lost in familiarity was compensated by a fresh look and a different way of doing business. CRAW-1 and turn-over briefs between RVAHs departing and arriving in the war zone provided a continuity of matters peculiar to the Vigilante community.

At the start of the RA-5C's first deployment, there was an official reluctance to send the expensive ($14 million apiece in 1960s money) and advanced technology (aeroplane, avionics and reconnaissance systems) Vigilante into high risk areas, so it was restricted to flights over South Vietnam and Laos. CVW-9 on USS *Ranger* (CVA-61) had a detachment of RF-8 Crusaders on board as 'insurance' for the unproven Vigilantes. Restrictions were lifted in early 1965, allowing RVAH-5 'Savage Sons' to fly the first RA-5C missions over North Vietnam.

Cooperation between the 'Light Photo' and 'Heavy Recce' units was excellent, with photographers-mates and related intelligence ratings sharing watches and work in the new IOIC.

USS *Ranger* and CVW-9 had cut short their training in the Hawaiian area because of the Tonkin Gulf

RVAH-5 Vigilante BuNo 151622 flies into the barricade aboard *Constellation* because of damage to its landing gear or tailhook. The barricade is made of vertical, thick, nylon straps. The upper and lower horizontal steel cables pull away from the stanchions and are fastened to an arresting gear engine to drag the aeroplane to a stop (*EBAL*)

incident and arrived on-the-line in mid-September. The first loss of an RA-5C in Vietnam, and the first aircraft loss for *Ranger*, came on 9 December 1964. Lt Cdr Donald Beard and Lt(jg) Brian Cronin were killed when BuNo 149306 (the first Vigilante produced as an RA-5C and not a conversion) crashed during a reconnaissance run in South Vietnam. The exact cause was never determined, although Lt Jim 'Pirate' Pirotte (then a junior pilot in RVAH-5, he later commanded RVAH-12, and finished with more time in the Vigilante than any other pilot) was lowered by helicopter sling into the jungle to investigate.

This RVAH-1 Vigilante is at tension on *Independence*'s catapult, its crew waiting for the catapult officer (left) to touch the deck as the final launch signal. Getting the RA-5C correctly positioned over the catapult prior to launching required subtlety and skill from both the pilot and the deck director. Vigilantes were frequently the last aircraft launched because they had plenty of fuel. This photograph was probably taken during training in early 1965, as there is a pylon on the wing and the flight deck crewmen are dressed for cold weather, not the tropical Gulf of Tonkin. The crest on the nose of AG 603 is unidentified (*EBAL*)

In April 1965 RVAH-5 turned over what they had learned to RVAH-1, which had arrived in the Tonkin Gulf aboard *Independence* for the Atlantic Fleet carrier's only time in combat.

Operation *Rolling Thunder*, launched on 2 March 1965, was intended to force North Vietnam to capitulate through air strikes of increasing intensity. What targets could be hit and which areas were off limits was determined in Washington, and not by local commanders. The specific targets that would require a major effort were on the A-list. A is Alpha in the phonetic alphabet, so attack missions using most of the aeroplanes in an air wing became known as Alpha strikes.

For the reconnaissance squadrons flying RF-8s and RA-5Cs, pre- and post-Alpha strike BDA photography became a major mission. During cyclic operations, route (roads, trails, waterways, railroads) reconnaissance was the equivalent of attack aircraft doing armed reconnaissance. Technically, such sorties into the North were called *Blue Trees* (Cuban missions over land had been *Blue Moons*). In addition, the RA-5C used SLR to make and update radar maps of Vietnam. The new A-6A Intruders used these to plan their night and all-weather attacks. Each RVAH squadron also had one or two aircraft PECM-capable, and they would run tracks along the borders of North Vietnam to locate enemy search and fire control radars.

A technician removes a film canister from a KA-51/53 series camera in one of the Vigilante's camera stations. Several major camera manufacturers supplied equipment of this type for the Vigilante (*Mersky*)

A new RA-5C cost $16 million in round, 1968 dollars. The oblique camera sight cost two cents. Until the jet's final years in the fleet, there was no mechanical means for the pilot to check that the road, river or coast he was photographing was centred. Instead, he had to carry a grease pencil. If the installed cameras were mounted at 37.5 degrees, en route to the target area he would roll to 37.5 degrees(!) on the attitude gyro and draw a line on the canopy along the horizon. This line would then tell the pilot whether the jet was too close or too far for optimum coverage.

RANs would monitor the distance for offset runs by slewing the TV camera 45 degrees to the side. Since imagery was clearer if the aeroplane was steady and wings level when the cameras fired, a good Vigilante pilot would time his jinking manoeuvres to come between exposures. The oblique cameras had a small green light on the pilot's glare shield that flashed when the cameras fired.

The RAN's ride during an offset oblique run was an exercise in sensory overload. In front of his face were two large round viewers. In one, the ground below, distorted by the lens, was moving past with yellow lines superimposed – these had to be watched to ensure the IMC was working. The other had a TV image of the target route, in hues of blue, moving past, but slanted at 45 degrees from level. Through the windows on either side, the real horizon was glimpsed as the jet banked from side to side. The rolling dials of the INS spun out position over the ground, and the RHAW gear was twinkling orange strobes of threat radars and making beeping noises. And this was all going on while the pilot was yanking and banking between pulses of the little green light.

One of the cameras that could be carried was the 18-inch focal-length panoramic. The million-dollar 18-inch pan was hugely sophisticated. It used a spinning prism to sweep from horizon to horizon, and could register a tennis ball from 20,000 ft. It also used film at a prodigious rate. Each exposure was five inches wide and 44 inches long. There was a smaller version of the panoramic camera with a three-inch focal length. The panoramic cameras were badly under-utilised, as they could have gotten coverage from safe distances. Tasking from higher commands, especially the USAF, demanded old-fashioned runs low over the target.

The usual camera configuration for 'route recce' was a tri-fan. The RA-5C had one camera aimed forward which ran for the entire mission. Its firing rate was slow and its photography used to recreate the route of flight. The other three cameras were a vertical, which shot straight down, and two oblique cameras aimed off to either side. Their angles could be set at 19.75, 37.5 or 52 degrees, depending on lens focal lengths. This resulted in overlapping, fan-shaped coverage of the ground below.

At the end of a flight, if weather and time of day permitted, the Vigilante would take photographs during a steady, level pass overhead the ship. The photography specialists would use known objects and markings on the carrier deck to calibrate the cameras.

Independence's route to war took ship and air wing from Norfolk, Virginia, around Africa, across the Indian Ocean and into the Tonkin Gulf in July 1965. The vessel's air wing, CVW-7, boasted the first A-6 Intruder unit in the fleet (VA-75) and RVAH-1, only the second RA-5C squadron to see combat. By now the mission emphasis was changing, as less than half the Vigilante flight crews were bomber qualified.

The deployment did not begin well, with three A-6s being lost due to faulty bomb fusing in the first month. The maps used to programme the Intruder's INS were also discovered to be erroneous, so the RA-5Cs were given the task of photo-mapping North Vietnam to update the system.

RVAH-1 lost its commanding officer on 20 July. Returning from a reconnaissance mission over North Vietnam, the crew successfully landed back aboard ship, only to discover that the arresting gear had been set incorrectly and the wire broke. RA-5C BuNo 151619 ran off the deck and into the water. There was no time to eject, and the pilot, Cdr Valentin Matula, and RAN, Lt Carl Gronquist, were killed on impact. Because of the aircraft's size and weight, arresting gear and catapults worked at maximum limits when operating with the Vigilante, and incorrect settings remained a problem throughout the jet's career.

John Smittle was an ensign RAN in RVAH-1 on this cruise (after another deployment as a RAN, Smittle went through pilot training, deployed in Skyhawks and was then a 'Vigi' pilot in RVAH-6), and he remembers flying into Tan Son Nhut air base, in South Vietnam, with the squadron XO to confer at the USAF reconnaissance centre – the Air Force were operating RF-101 Voodoos. USAF centralised control of intelligence assets would become a sore spot for the Navy, as the centre's information was usually out of date, while on-the-spot intelligence from Vigilantes and IOIC was not considered 'official'.

Blue Tree became the designation for reconnaissance missions into North Vietnam, and a new target was added to the Vigilante's list. SA-2 'Guideline' SAM sites had been under construction, and in July, 1965 they began launching missiles against US aircraft. Film from the RA-5C's array of cameras was scrutinised for the distinctive six-sided SAM sites, while the PECM located 'Fan Song' guidance radars electronically.

The first Vigilante to be shot down in Vietnam, on 16 October 1965, had been searching for SA-2 sites when, near Hon Gay, doing 650 knots, BuNo 151615 was hit in the tail by either AAA or a SAM. After the flight controls failed the crew, pilot Lt Cdr James Bell and RAN Lt Cdr 'Duffy' Hutton ejected and landed near one of the small islands off the coast. They both climbed into their survival rafts, but were picked up by fishermen in sampans and captured. After repatriation in 1973, Bell told of being tied to the sampan's mast, which struck him as ironic as the night before he had watched the 1946 movie *Two Years Before the Mast*!

The next day, three F-4 Phantom IIs from *Independence* were lost on an Alpha strike against the Thai Nguyen bridge north of Hanoi. The RA-5C

RVAH-7 RA-5C BuNo 151629 has its tanks topped off by a buddy store-equipped A-4C of VA-76 during CVW-9's combat deployment aboard *Enterprise* in 1965-66 (*Mersky*)

covering the attack returned to the carrier unharmed.

RVAH-1 had taken six aircraft on the deployment, and their losses were not replaced. The squadron had used flasher pods at night, but gave these up due to significant AAA. RVAH-1 also used both three- and eighteen-inch panoramic cameras to get some stand-off distance as the North Vietnamese air defences grew stronger.

Lt(jg) Dave Sharp (left) and Lt Cdr Jack Tuttle (right) of RVAH-7 are escorted up *Enterprise's* flight deck by a flight surgeon on 27 September 1964. Another aeroplane flying in formation with this crew had reported seeing hydraulic fluid leaking from A-5A BuNo 147863. Tuttle dropped the ram air turbine for emergency power, but with the fluid gone, he moved the stick only twice and the controls froze. The crew ejected moments later. *Enterprise* had sent up a formation of 40 aircraft to perform a fly-past for the people of Recife, in Brazil, on the carrier's way home from the Operation *Sea Orbit* around-the-world cruise. Seen here moments after being flown back to CVAN-65, pilot and RAN are still wearing their Mk 3C flotation gear, with the bright yellow bladders inflated. In 1968 the Navy changed to LPA type equipment, which added a 'horse collar' float to keep the survivor's head upright. In 1978 Cdr Dave Sharp was the commanding officer of RVAH-7 on the squadron's penultimate deployment (*Sharp*)

Enterprise had been home-ported in Norfolk, Virginia, across the James River from Newport News Shipbuilding Corporation, where the first nuclear-powered carrier had been built. In anticipation of the growing conflict in South-east Asia, the vessel was transferred to the Pacific Fleet, and it would be based in Alameda, California. The carrier changed ports via the war zone, and it did not reach Alameda for nine months. For the ship's crew, and the men of CVW-9, which included RVAH-7, this meant a long voyage east around Africa, across the Indian Ocean and through the Straits of Malacca to the naval air station at Cubi Point, in the Philippines. Time in port was short, and when supplies and ammunition had been loaded, *Enterprise* headed for the Tonkin Gulf, and the newly designated spot in the ocean called *Yankee Station*.

The 'Peacemakers' were familiar with *Enterprise*, having made the first Vigilante deployment aboard the vessel as VAH-7 flying A3Js – that 1962 cruise to the Mediterranean was also the first for CVAN-65 and for the F4H Phantom II. After an interruption of six months for the Cuban Missile Crisis, VAH-7 went back on board once the carrier returned to the Mediterranean, and then participated in the around-the-world nuclear-powered demonstration voyage. Upon returning to NAS Sanford after Operation *Sea Orbit*, the unit transitioned to the RA-5C and was redesignated RVAH-7.

On *Yankee Station*, *Enterprise* and *Independence* steamed side by side for a turnover of special equipment, unexpended ordnance and, most importantly, lessons learned. RVAH-1 passed on its hard-won knowledge to RVAH-7.

LANDING ON THE SHIP

The following description of landing on an aircraft carrier provides a look at what Vigilante pilots faced at the end of every mission;

'Usually, the Vigilante flies into the break alone – and fast. Downwind, lower the flaps to a full 50 degrees, lower the gear and have the RAN check by TV what the indicator is saying. The heavy, A-frame tailhook is

A 'markingless' RVAH-1 Vigilante is seen just seconds before launching from *Independence* in 1965. The holdback and bridle are tight, the flaps are fully down, horizontal 'slabs' at the correct angle and fully opened afterburners brighten the twilight. A quirk of the RA-5C was the cockpit air-conditioning cut out when the flaps were lowered due to all the engine bleed-air being diverted to the leading edge boundary-layer control ducts (*Woodul*)

lowered by a lever on the right side of the cockpit. As the flaps come down, so do the leading edge slats, and the cockpit air conditioning cuts out as engine bleed air is diverted over the wing. As the airspeed slows toward 155 knots, the angle-of-attack indexer on the glare shield lights up. Engage the auto-throttles with a switch. Check auto-throttle operation by pulling back on the stick – the throttles move forward. Push the stick and the throttles move back. There may have been lots of fuel out flying around, but at a max trap weight of 50,000 lbs there's only enough for four "looks at the deck". Not a time to screw-up with the entire ship watching and waiting for you to trap.

'Across the wake, pick up the meatball. Wings level when on the landing centreline. Start the landing scan you first learned in Pensacola – meatball, line-up, angle-of-attack; meatball, line-up, angle-of-attack. In the Vigilante, you fly the ball with small, tiny, tweaks of the stick to keep it dead centre. Gentle touches with fingers and thumb. An exact description borders on the sexual. The auto-throttles keep the speed correct, their jerky movements reassuring. Nevertheless, your left hand rests on the throttles all the time . . . just in case. Line-up has to be solved early. A turn to line-up an RA-5C means the spoilers come up and their drag will pull the nose down if not anticipated.

'Close-in, your scan changes as angle-of-attack becomes less important, then the line-up drops out. For the last seconds, it is all meatball, meatball, meatball. Touchdown has to be in a perfect attitude or there is the risk of a shattered nose wheel or the tailhook slamming up into the fuselage. On a good trap at Vigilante approach speeds, you are thrown forward hard against your straps (woe betide those who forget to lock their harness), and you have to struggle to bring the throttles to idle, raise the flaps, press the button on the stick for nose wheel steering, switch hands to raise the tailhook, switch hands to advance the power, switch hands again to fold the wings and taxi out of the landing area.

'Taxying the jet was unique because the nose wheel was eight feet behind the pilot. It took some getting used to even in normal turns, and on the ship there were situations that required the nose wheel to be run up to the edge of the deck with the pilot watching the director over his shoulder and the RAN looking at water in the viewfinder. To the relief of crews, this will eventually be forbidden at night, and discouraged in daylight.'

HOT TIMES

The basic pattern for the naval air campaign in the Vietnam War was set in March 1965 with the start of *Rolling Thunder* missions – *Blue Trees* for reconnaissance aeroplanes. 1966, 1967 and part of 1968 saw the targets change with the whims and political perceptions of the Johnson administration. The North Vietnamese defences varied as new equipment arrived, and the opportunity to regroup and rearm came with each pause in the bombing.

The pattern for the carriers in the Tonkin Gulf was set with schedule designations as Red, White or Blue. When there were three carriers available, as was usually the case, one ship would fly from Midnight to Noon (Red), another from 0600 to 1800 hrs (White) and the third from Noon to Midnight (Blue). This gave each air wing/ship team a 12-hour flying period, while providing double coverage during daylight hours. Cyclic ops were the norm, with aircraft launching and recovering every one-and-a-half hours.

When Alpha strikes were called for, all aircraft would be launched and recovered after the strike, before either launching another Alpha or resuming a cyclic pattern. There were exceptions and variations to this pattern because of the need to replenish food, fuel and ordnance every six or seven days, the size of the carrier and composition of the embarked air wing and carriers leaving the line for R&R in port or returning home.

For the RVAH squadrons, daylight missions were 'route recces' along designated stretches of roads, trails, railways, waterways, or pre- and post-strike photography for the Alpha strikes. At night, initial attempts at photography with flasher pods proved unsuitable – not because the imagery was bad, but because the pulses of bright light from the three million candle-power strobes made the Vigilante an easy target for the anti-aircraft gunners.

As the number of guns in the country increased, night flasher missions became highly hazardous. Fortunately the installation of the IR mapping sensor (designated AAS-21) from 1968 onwards made it unnecessary to use flashers to detect the heavy traffic moving southwards in the darkness. The IR sensor had the added advantage of being able to detect targets that photography could not. The AAS-21 recorded temperature differential, and could 'see through' vegetation that had been cut and put over trucks and storage as camouflage. The IR was run on all missions, being supplemental in the day and the primary sensor at night.

Also at night, crews would fly PECM and SLR missions, usually in combination. Although these systems would be run during day flights, they both depended on steady, wings-level flying for best results. SLR was installed in all RA-5Cs, the rear two-thirds of the belly canoe housing antennas, power supplies and recorders for the system. In addition to providing intelligence – boats, ships and trains showed up especially well – SLR gave the Intruder and, later, Corsair II crews a current radar picture to use in their planning for attacks in bad weather or at night.

PECM (AN/ALQ-161) was a special installation that went into what would have been the weapons bay of the A3J bomber. In the RA-5C, the PECM replaced one of the fuel cans. Each RVAH squadron had one or two aircraft PECM-configured, and an Air Intelligence (AI) officer specialising in PECM assigned. A close look at a Vigilante shows square antenna panels scattered along the fuselage sides. However, since the panels are painted the same as the rest of the aircraft, they are not usually noticeable. Additional antennas are in the wing leading edges – apparent as dielectric material in the stainless steel. All Vigilantes had the antennas, so the PECM 'can' could be installed as needed.

The INS, backed up by the RANs log, provided an accurate position of the RA-5C to the PECM. Upon returning to the ship, the magnetic tapes were taken to a machine in the IOIC, where they were read, and the location of radar and electronic emitters like tracking and fire control radars were automatically printed on a map The PECM also recorded the pulse-repetition frequency, band width and other parameters that enabled the AIs to determine exactly what type and model radar it was. The two primary PECM tracks were north and south along the borders of North Vietnam – the Black Track over Laos and the Blue Track over the Gulf of Tonkin.

1965 ENDS

The end of 1965 saw three RVAH squadrons on-the-line – the 'Bats' of RVAH-13 aboard USS *Kitty Hawk* (CVA-63) and the 'Peacemakers' of RVAH-7 on *Enterprise*, both having arrived in October, and the 'Hooters' of RVAH-9 on *Ranger*, which joined the line in December. That same month RVAH-1 headed back home aboard *Independence*.

RVAH-9 had previously deployed to the Mediterranean aboard USS *Saratoga* (CVA-60) for its first time out with the RA-5C in 1964-65, RVAH-13 was newly transitioned from the A-3 Skywarrior, and RVAH-7 had completed three previous cruises with *Enterprise* equipped with A3J-1/A-5As. The latter unit was back aboard CVAN-65 once again, but this time with the RA-5C.

Enterprise began by operating down south from *Dixie Station* (a usual practice, as it gave newly-arrived air wings a chance to adjust to combat flying and the pace of operations), and on 15 December 1965 it lost RA-5C BuNo 151633 in an area Navy jets rarely flew over – the far west coast of South Vietnam. The search was for 'Wiblicks' (Water Borne Logistics Craft, WBLC, was the fancy, official designation for boats, barges, sampans, etc.) amid the coastal swamps. Pilot Lt J K Sutor and RAN Lt(jg) G B Dresser were flying at 3500 ft over the bay of Vinh Cay Duong when they felt a thump and their cockpits filled with smoke. The pilot killed the electric flight system and fought the controls until, ten miles over the Gulf of Siam, the crew were forced to eject.

The nearest rescuer was a US Army UH-1B Huey helicopter, which was vectored to the crash site. A sampan was approaching the survivors, and because its identity and intentions were unclear, the Huey pilot had the Navy aircraft holding overhead fire a burst of 20 mm cannon in front of the vessel to warn it off. As there was no hoist on the UH-1B, the pilot skillfully hovered with his landing skid on the water. First Sutor and then Dresser climbed into the helicopter and were flown to safety.

When they were returned to the ship several days later, Cdr Ken Enney, CO of RVAH-7, gave them a chewing-out. It was bad enough, he said, that they were sent out to look for such insignificant targets, but to lose an expensive and sophisticated aeroplane while wandering around 'sight-seeing' was intolerable. Sutor ejected again in October from BuNo 149288 while *Enterprise* was back operating off the California coast.

Although the RA-5C had a sophisticated navigation system, pilots always had a map with course lines for the reconnaissance route drawn on it as a visual back-up in case of ASB-12 failures. A junior RAN in RVAH-7 who flew with the CO made up his skipper's maps for him. As trips over North Vietnam became routine, the ensign RAN would simply add another set of lines and headings, rather than re-drawing the entire chart with AAA and SAM envelopes. During a port visit in Japan, he bought a set of 24 coloured pencils. Back on the line, he used a different colour for each mission, until after the tenth he told his CO to 'follow the mauve line today'. The commander crumpled the well-worn map, threw it over the side and demanded a fresh one!

In late 1965, Lt(jg) Dave Sharp (later CO of RVAH-7) was in the back of a 'Peacemakers' Vigilante heading north from *Dixie Station*, and about to turn into Vietnam, when the RA-5C did not turn the direction Sharp called for and the pilot, Lt Cdr Jerry Chapdelaine, would not answer his increasingly frantic calls over the intercom. Sharp correctly guessed that his pilot was hypoxic from an oxygen system malfunction;

'That's when I started calling him every name I could think of, along with "dive, dive, dive". Then, when he did push over, I thought we wouldn't pull out. My call became "pull-out, pull-out, pull-out, you SOB". When he finally did, we kept going slower and slower, so I started yelling, "power, power, power!" By this time we were at 8000 ft or so, and Jerry was beginning to sound normal. Apparently, when he attached his mask on climb-out it was not tight enough. When he started losing consciousness, he slumped forward and forced his mask on enough to keep him at a semi-conscious state. He later told me that all he could remember was hearing me call him various foul names, and he just

RVAH-13 RA-5C BuNo 151627 waits its turn to be launched off catapult one aboard *Kitty Hawk* in the Gulf of Tonkin in early 1966. This aircraft survived the carnage of the 'Bats' first combat deployment, only to fall victim to AAA during the unit's second cruise on 9 March 1967. Squadron CO, Cdr Charles Putnam, was lost, but RAN, Lt(jg) Frank Prendergast, dramatically seized his freedom after briefly being captured (*Mersky*)

wanted to catch me and kill me. I told him that I'd had a few similar thoughts about him myself.'

The 'Bats' of RVAH-13 had a rough start on *Kitty Hawk's* first combat deployment. The Uong Bi thermal power plant north of Haiphong had been the target for multiple air wing attacks on 20 December 1965, and two Vigilantes, with F-4 escorts, were assigned to get BDA photographs. The escorts and the other Vigilante lost sight and radio contact with 'Flint River 604' (BuNo 151624) at about the time the jet was due over the target area. The coast near Hon Gai was searched without finding any wreckage or sign of Lt Cdr Guy Johnson or Lt(jg) Lee Nordahl.

Two days later, 'Flint River 603' (BuNo 151632) was after pre-strike photography of the railway bridge at Hai Duong for the next day's strike. Flying at 3000 ft between cloud layers, RAN Lt(jg) Glenn Daigle saw bursting AAA and heard the Vigilante hit several times. The RA-5C went into gyrations, and because the pilot was not answering over the intercom, Daigle had to assume his pilot, Lt Cdr Max Lukenbach, had been hit and was unconscious, or worse. There was an explosion and Daigle ejected – he does not remember pulling the face-curtain or alternate ejection handles. He was a PoW until released in February 1973.

A hard-earned lesson was to never fly above a cloud layer if there was the slightest chance of SAMs. The primary tactic to avoid the SA-2 was a diving, rolling turn toward the missile. Being above clouds reduced the time available to spot and evade the SAM. Many crews forgot or ignored this rule to their dismay.

Days after these losses, President Johnson, at Secretary of Defense McNamara's urging, declared a 37-day bombing halt over the start of the new year. Pilots reported that at night the Ho Chi Minh Trail looked like the New Jersey Turnpike during rush hour. The North Vietnamese did not begin negotiations as futilely hoped, but used the time to build up their air defences to a formidable level.

Lt Jerry Coffee had flown RF-8s over Cuba during the missile crisis in 1962, and instructed in the Vigilante RAG before joining RVAH-13. On 3 February 1966, days after the bombing halt had ended, he was on a 'road recce' between Vinh and Thanh Hoa when he was hit by AAA during a second pass over the same section of highway.

Another hard-earned lesson for any aircraft in a hostile area was no multiple runs over the same target. Lt Coffee headed for the water, but less than a mile offshore his 'Vigi' (BuNo 151625) broke apart and he and Lt(jg) Robert Hanson ejected. Coffee was hauled aboard a fishing boat and spent the next seven years as a PoW. He had seen his RAN land in the water, but Lt(jg) Hanson was never heard from again. The North Vietnamese later said that

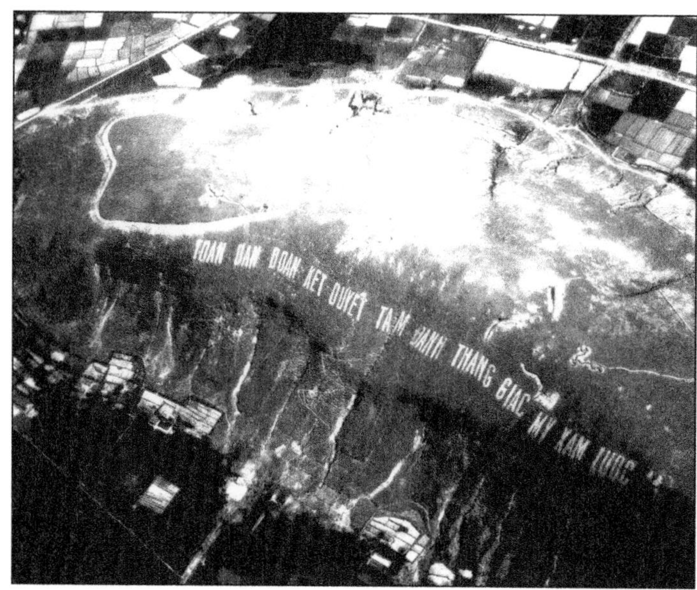

Lt Cdr Al Wattay and Lt Jim 'Bones' Morgan (a former enlisted BN) of RVAH-13 caught this image of a karst hill while on a mission to the MiG base at Kep, deep in North Vietnam. The legend translates as 'Victoriously Strike the Encroaching American Bandits'. The hill's value was not only for propaganda, as the bare areas on the top are heavy AAA emplacements (*Wattay*)

Hanson had died from his wounds and was buried on the beach. After repatriation in 1973, Coffee did the illustrations for Cdr Howard Rutledge's book on the PoW experience, *In the Presence of Mine Enemies*.

Despite losses, RVAH-13 was instrumental in one of the most effective strikes of the early war. The Alpha target list system had recently been put into effect. While most strikes were specified by Washington, local commanders were allowed to choose some targets, but they had to get permission. Capt Martin D 'Red' Carmody was captain of *Kitty Hawk*, and an early supporter of the RA-5C. In April, when a 'Bat' Vigilante came back from a coastal reconnaissance run with photographs of a new, large, coal loading complex near the port of Cam Pha, he saw an opportunity to hurt the enemy's war effort. The strike became a perfect example of how the on-the-spot intelligence capability of the IOIC has always been used.

Timing was everything. In collusion with Carrier Task Force 77 Chief-of-staff Capt 'Jig Dog' Ramage, a squadronmate of Carmody's from World War 2, *Kitty Hawk* launched a pre-dawn strike of eight bombed-up F-4s and six A-6s, each with 6000 lbs of ordnance, plus support aircraft. Capt Carmody sent the message that 'unless otherwise directed', they were going to bomb the coal facility at a time of day when he knew the response in Washington would be slow. The ship's communication officer was also carefully briefed to take his time delivering the reply when it came. The strike group had pulled off the target and the RVAH-13 RA-5C had gone in for BDA when the cease and desist message arrived . . . too late.

Ranger had been operating on *Dixie Station* for just 24 hours when, on 16 January 1966, RVAH-9 Vigilante BuNo 149312 crashed after what should have been a routine touch-and-go landing on the ship. The starboard engine exploded when full throttle was applied and the aeroplane crashed into the sea with the loss of Lt Cdr Charles Schoonover and Ens Hal Hollingsworth. It would be the only RA-5C the 'Hooters' would lose in two combat deployments.

BuNo 149312 had completed a reconnaissance flight over South Vietnam before returning to *Ranger*, and the fateful touch-and-go. A frustration with such incidents was the fact that it will never be know if the aeroplane crashed because it had been hit by unseen and unfelt small arms fire that only took effect later in the flight.

The US Navy's primary reconnaissance sources fly together during a mission from *Ranger* in 1965, when the RA-5C was unproven and the RF-8 was embarked as a form of 'insurance'. After this deployment, the RF-8s operated from the smaller decks and the Vigilantes from the 'supercarriers' which had IOICs. This RA-5C (BuNo 149312) went out again the next year on *Ranger* with RVAH-9, and on the second day on-line it crashed after what should have been a routine touch-and-go landing on the ship. The crew was lost with the aeroplane. It would be the only RA-5C that RVAH-9 would lose in two combat deployments (*EBAL*)

The wing of an A-4 Skyhawk loaded with two 19-shot 2.75-in folding fin rocket pods frames an RVAH-6 Vigilante on the deck of *Ranger* in the hectic days of late 1966. The portion of the canoe housing the SLR is swung down and the number four sensor station is empty, awaiting the installation of a module with loaded cameras (*EBAL*)

'Hooter' flight crews became frustrated when, after doing all the planning for the first reconnaissance flights into Hanoi and Haiphong in coordination with USAF strikes, they were ordered to turn over their plans to RVAH-6 when the latter arrived in-theatre as part of CVW-15 aboard USS *Constellation* (CVA-64) in June 1966. The 'Fleurs' got to fly the missions instead.

Lt Bob 'Bull' Davis (his nickname was earned by hitting the bulls-eye 13 times as a bombardier-navigator with VAH-6 when it flew A-3 Skywarriors) had made the transition to the RA-5C with the squadron. He stated;

'I don't remember that the "Hooters'" flight planning was used verbatim by us when we arrived. I am certain we used the intel on SAM and AAA sites that they had gathered, but we laid out our own targets and routes. Turnovers like that were important. At the end of our stay we passed on a lot to "Recce Seven".'

The first CO of the 'Fleurs' as RVAH-6 was Cdr C R 'Screaming Charlie' Smith, who claimed 'Tracers won't hurt you. They just bounce off'. He later commanded RVAH-3 .

At this stage of the Vietnam War the US Navy was concerned about increasing MiG activity, and it decided to try a USAF-inspired camouflage scheme that would make its aeroplanes more difficult for high flying enemy fighters to detect. All types of aircraft were painted, including those of RVAH-6, -11, -12 and -13. Jets were camouflaged in shades of green and brown on the uppersurfaces, the patterns and colours varying depending on where the repainting was done. RVAH-6 had its

The six flight crews of RVAH-6 embarked on *Constellation* in 1966. The RANs are kneeling and the paired pilots are standing behind them. Typical of the RVAH squadrons of the time, there are two commander- (CO and XO) and four lieutenant commander-rank pilots, while there is one lieutenant commander RAN, four lieutenants and one lieutenant (junior grade). Those mentioned elsewhere in this book are, RANs, third from left, Lt Cdr George Schneider (a former enlisted BN), fourth from left, Lt Doug Cook (who later commanded an EA-6B squadron) and far right, Lt Wayne 'Tiny' Mulholland (who flew two combat cruises without a scratch, but was killed in 1975 in the Mediterranean with RVAH-11 in a landing accident). Amongst the pilots, standing second from left is Lt Cdr Harry Klein (who later commanded RVAH-5), third from left is the CO, Cdr Ed Feeks (later CRAW-1), far right, Lt Cdr Larry DeBoxtel (who next became the 'Recce RAG' LSO), and second from right, Lt Cdr Bob Dean (who would go to *WestPac* again as XO of RVAH-12, and eventually be the last Commander of CRAW-1) (*Wells*)

RVAH-6 Vigilante BuNo 149313, freshly painted in a temporary camouflage of green and dark-green in 1966 at NAS North Island. The dark paint made the aircraft more visible to AAA gunners, so the idea was dropped. Although no RA-5Cs remained painted this way for very long, the 'Cami-Vigis' have received a disproportionate amount of coverage in books and magazines the world over (*EBAL*)

aeroplanes resprayed at the Overhaul and Repair Facility at NAS North Island, in San Diego, before embarking on *Constellation*.

The green Vigilantes undertook the usual work-ups in Hawaii and during the trip to Japan and Subic Bay, in the Philippines. After the first Tonkin Gulf line period, and the air wing's loss of an F-4 Phantom II, an A-6 Intruder and four A-4 Skyhawks – all to ground fire – the water-based camouflage paint was removed by sailors with solvent-soaked rags. RVAH-6 aeroplanes remained the standard gull-grey and white from then on. Despite the bad experiences of the *Constellation* squadrons, the camouflage idea was tried again later, with the same results.

Dick Wells went to sea three times with early RA-5C squadrons as a technical representative for North American;

'All RVAH-6 aeroplanes were over-painted at North Island prior to the cruise. They had expected more air intercepts, and after the first line period the camouflage was removed. The finish was very rough – it had almost a sandy feel – and it reduced the maximum air speed by 20 knots or more. One thing the paint was good for was over-G inspections. Any loose fastener or loose panels would clearly show up due to the coloured paint being rubbed away. If I remember correctly, only the CO had prior combat experience from Korea, and everyone else had to acquire the "jinking" expertise. We could sure see where the spoiler/deflector had contacted the edges, as they would close while the wings were still bending. The star and bar insignia, side number and BuNo on the vertical fin were also applied much smaller that normal on the camouflaged jets. I was told that this was done to distort distance indications for attacking Vietnamese MiG pilots.'

Lt 'Bull' Davis was crewed with Lt 'Gigi' Gretter for the 'Fleurs'' first combat deployment with the Vigilante. During a mission to get the results of an air wing strike on the Dong Son petroleum storage site near Haiphong, they had a flight control malfunction and the RA-5C began to lose height. While Gretter handled the jet, Davis kept the cameras running properly. Despite SAM near-misses and

There are two possible explanations as to why this camouflaged Vigilante features full colour unit markings for RVAH-11 – a unit that, officially at least, did not participate in the tactical paint trials of early 1966. It was either another attempt at applying the scheme to a fleet jet, or it was an RA-5C transferred in from RVAH-13, which had painted its jets in a similar pattern of greens and brown. Either way, leaving the black and white checkerboard on the tail was at odds with trying to make the jet inconspicuous (*Mersky*)

One of RVAH-13's camouflaged RA-5Cs cruises over Vietnamese jungle in the early spring of 1966. When viewed from above, the three-tone tactical paint scheme was very effective, but the greatest danger facing these aircraft was from AAA and SAMs, not from MiGs. Indeed, camouflaged aircraft were more conspicuous when viewed from the ground. Conversely, they became virtually invisible on the deck during night operations (*Mersky*)

intensified flak because of their dangerously low altitude, they made it to 'feet wet' safely, and with photographic intelligence that went beyond the intended coverage – a typical mission for the Vigilante.

Squadronmates Lt Cdr Art Skelly and his RAN, Lt(jg) Joe Shevlin, survived one of the strangest events of the Vigilante's career. In 1980, then Capt Skelly wrote;

'The Vigilante had the dubious distinction of photographing targets before and after the strike group bombed it. The Vietnamese were always waiting for the BDA pass after the last attack aircraft pulled off the target.

'Of the 260 combat flights I flew in the Vigilante, the most unusual had to be with RVAH-6 in July 1966 aboard *Constellation*. One dark, overcast Sunday morning, we photographed an oil storage area that had been hit the previous night by A-6s. On our way out of the target area over downtown Haiphong, we attracted some severe AAA, automatic weapons fire and SAMs. Tracers were crisscrossing over the canopy and the F-4 escort was going crazy calling out flak. I decided that we had had enough, so I pulled up into a nearby thunderstorm to get away from the heaviest flak I had ever seen.

'It didn't work. Not only did we immediately encounter rain, hail and lightning, but the tracers were streaking around us and there were bright flashes from lightning and exploding shells. I couldn't tell whether the turbulence was violent because of near misses or the storm! The attitude gyro didn't look quite right, but that was the least of my worries then. We soon popped out of the storm cell and I realised the gyro *was* correct – not only were we upside down, but the F-4 was right there in position, also inverted!

In 1966, RVAH-6's Lt Cdr Art Skelly and Lt Joe Shevlin had a unique thrill upon launching from *Constellation* when, as they shot off the bow, the pilot heard a loud boom and looked in his mirror in time to see the rear canopy sailing past the tail. The Air Boss on CVA-64 thought that Shevlin had ejected, and he sent the plane-guard helicopter over to search for him. Despite the wind noise, and after an almost comical exchange on the intercom, the crew figured out that they were each okay, and the Vigilante flyable. Skelly slowed the jet down, dumped fuel to get to landing weight, came around and landed. A photographer on the LSO platform took this picture of the 'topless Vigi'. They were flying camouflaged RA-5C BuNo 149313 NL 702 (*Skelly*)

"Do you think, Comrade, that Hanoi will believe it?"
from an original drawing by McMillan

In the thick of the action again in July 1966, Lt Cdr Skelly and Lt Shevlin incurred the wrath of Haiphong Harbour's AAA and SAM during a challenging BDA 'photo recce' mission. The pilot pulled up into a thunderstorm in an effort to evade the enemy's attention, and turbulence promptly flipped the Vigilante upside down. When they emerged inverted from the storm cloud, their F-4 Phantom II escort was still on their wing – also upside down. The rest of RVAH-6 threatened to mount a camera on the top of Skelly's helmet for any such future manoeuvres. The story was soon all over the ship, and talented jet mechanic ADJ3 Macmillan drew this cartoon, which was widely circulated (*Skelly*)

'Joe recognised that the nose had fallen through, and was telling me to pull out. I rolled level and pulled hard because the water was awfully close. Joe said that the radar altimeter had gone to zero before we started to climb.

'There was a large merchant ship in front of us – it turned out to be Chinese – and as we flew past, our escort Phantom II called that a machine gun on the stern was firing *down* at us.

'Once back on the ship, I had maintenance check the "Vigi" for overstress and battle damage. Despite some of the heaviest flak I had ever seen, there wasn't a single hole in the aeroplane!

'The guys in the ready room threatened to mount a Brownie camera on top of my hardhat for future manoeuvres.'

A fortnight later, this same crew was again over Haiphong when three large flashes of AAA exploded in front of their nose. Lt(jg) Shevlin lost his radar and navigation system, but got the photographs. Back onboard *Constellation*, a series of shrapnel holes were discovered from one side of the fuselage to the other, just inches in front of Lt Cdr Skelly's feet.

On 19 August 1966, RVAH-6's Lt Cdr Jim Thompson and his RAN, Lt(jg) G Parten, were on a road reconnaissance northwest of Vinh when AAA opened up and their Vigilante (BuNo 149309) suddenly rolled. With only partial control, Thompson headed for the coast. The Phantom II escort reported a fire in the jet's wheel-well area, and that sections of the left wing were breaking off. When the nose pitched over, both crewmen ejected at extremely high speed.

Thompson later said that time compression then kicked in, and when his eyes peered over the top of the windshield into the slipstream, he wanted to reverse-vector back into the cockpit! His ride was particularly violent, and he was badly bruised with his flight suit in tatters. The pilot landed in a marshy area close to the shore, and despite suffering from a dislocated shoulder, he avoided capture by staying underwater in the reeds and breathing through a plastic tube he kept in his sock. A searching Vietnamese soldier stepped on his leg but he must have thought that it was a log, for he moved off. At nightfall Thompson swam and drifted with the tide until he was far enough out to sea to be picked up by a helicopter. Lt(jg) Parten was rescued by a Navy ship.

Thompson and Parten were some of the few successful survivors of a supersonic ejection. Although the North American HS-1 ejection seat was designed for employment above Mach 1, the design assumed that the occupant would be wearing a full pressure-suit for protection, and that arm restraints would be installed. The ejection seat had bars that came down on top of the crewman's feet, pads that rose up under and panels alongside the knees to restrain his legs and a cord fastened near both wrists that would pull tight and keep the arms from flailing. The arm restraint proved awkward to wear, however, and it was soon discarded in the fleet.

The original seat was good to a speed as slow as 100 knots, and this was later improved to a zero-zero capability with the advent of the HS-1A seat in the RA-5C. A face curtain with a hefty metal handle was considered the primary means of ejecting. The alternate method was to turn and pull either of the two handles near the crewman's knees.

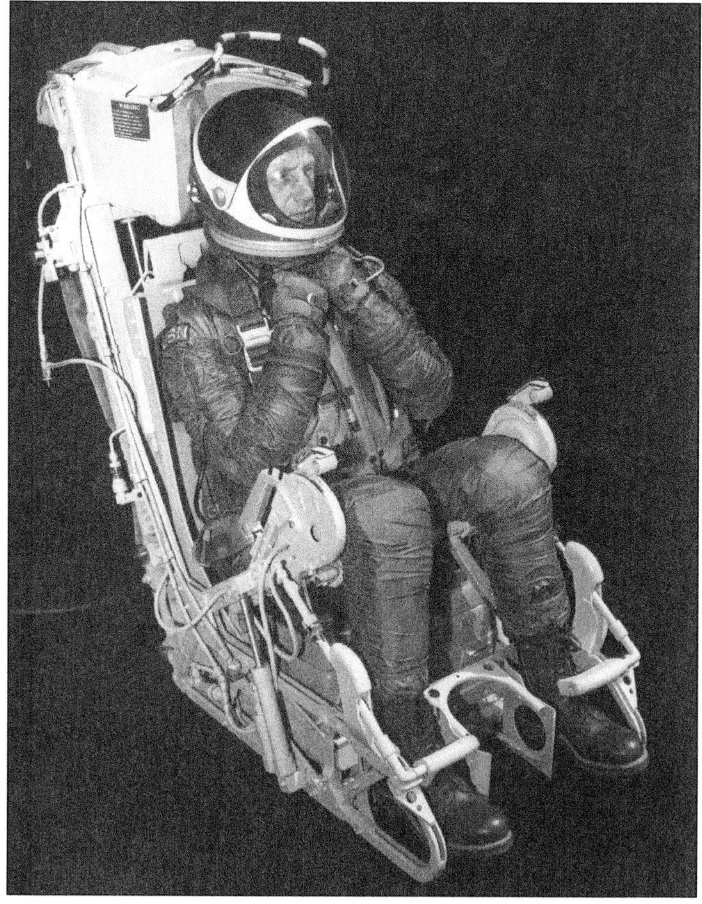

A pilot demonstrates how the Vigilante's HS-1 ejection seat would appear as it rode up the rails – the knee risers are up, the foot restraints are down and the crewman's arms pulled in tight. He is wearing a B F Goodrich Mk IV full-pressure suit (*EBAL*)

22 October 1966 was a bad day for CVW-15 aboard CVA-64. Firstly, an F-4B Phantom II of VF-161 was shot down north of Thanh Hoa. The next launch from *Constellation* included RVAH-6 Vigilante BuNo 150830 and another Phantom II for a route reconnaissance flight between Hanoi and Hai Duong. The escorting F-4 was hit by ground fire and began a turn back to the nearest coast. As the RA-5C turned to follow, its pilot, Lt Cdr Thomas Kolstad, called a SAM launch. The crew of the F-4B lost sight of the 'Vigi'. The fate of the RA-5C and its crew, Kolstad and Lt(jg) William Kienert, remained a mystery until a Vietnamese report was released which stated that the aircraft had been shot down by an SA-2 and the crew had ejected at very low altitude and been killed.

One week later *Constellation* headed east, and it was home by Christmas. 1966 ended with only two RVAH squadrons on the line – RVAH-7 on *Enterprise* and RVAH-13 on *Kitty Hawk*. Both were unusual for having stayed with the same ship for consecutive deployments. Indeed, this would happen only once more during the war.

In a curious event while undertaking a training mission, pilots Lt Cdrs Al Wattay and Bob Kuhlke found themselves going in opposite directions one night. The result was this photograph, taken by the light from an underwing flasher pod. The powerful strobe light stopped motion, even though the aircraft had a relative speed of over 600 mph. The lights on the wingtips show as a streak. The flasher pod, fitted with three strobe lights, was installed on the left wing. They could be carried on either wing, and were powered by a wind-driven generator at the back end of the pod (*Wattay*)

Enterprise's first combat loss during its second cruise was RA-5C BuNo 151623 of RVAH-7, which was lost on 12 February 1967. The Vigilante and its escort were flying at 500 ft and 560 knots 30 miles northeast of Thanh Hoa when they ran into a heavy barrage of AAA and the RA-5C was hit in the right wing. The jet just made it to the coast near the mouth of the Red River, where Cdr C H 'Pinky' Jarvis and Lt(jg) P M Artlip ejected at high speed and were battered by the wind stream.

The infamous bridge at Thanh Hoa. This photograph was taken on the last day of operations – 14 May – for RVAH-13 during the 1967 deployment on *Kitty Hawk*. Note the photo data block on the lower left corner of the print (*Wattay*)

An immediate, large-scale search and rescue (SAR) effort began to protect and save the pilot and RAN. An E-2A Hawkeye coordinated the actions of four F-4B Phantom IIs, four A-1H Skyraiders, two SH-3 'Big Mother' helicopters and a USAF HU-16 Albatross amphibious aircraft, as well a Navy destroyer. During the rescue, a North Vietnamese patrol boat sped along the coast in an attempt to capture the downed aircrew. One of the Phantom IIs fired a Sparrow air-to-air missile at the enemy boat, which turned and fled, probably damaged. The pilot was rescued by the Albatross and the RAN hoisted into a helicopter.

On 9 March 1967, RVAH-13 RAN Lt(jg) Frank Prendergast became the only American aviator to escape after being captured in North Vietnam. His story was almost too incredible to be true.

Prendergast had gone through the RAG with Lt Cdr Al Wattay, and they continued as a tactical crew in RVAH-13. However, Lt Jim 'Bones' Morgan (a former enlisted BN, and among the most decorated LDOs in the Navy) had gone home on emergency leave so the 'Bats'' commanding officer, Cdr Charles Putnam, needed a RAN. That afternoon he chose Lt(jg) Prendergast to accompany him on a coastal reconnaissance mission. Normally flown between 3000 and 5000 ft, with a two- to three-mile displacement offshore, Cdr Putnam violated hard-learned rules about altitudes and cloud layers in a desire to get the tasked coverage.

Near Long Chau, 30 miles northwest of Thanh Hoa, Cdr Putnam dove 'Flint River 605' (BuNo 151627) down to 350 ft less than a quarter-mile off the beach to start their run up the coastline. Hit by small-arms fire from the ground, the Vigilante burst into flames and became uncontrollable. Putnam initiated ejection for both crewmembers. While it is most likely that the CO did not eject successfully, he was officially listed as missing in action based on a report from the escort aircraft that a Navy pilot may have been seen running from armed soldiers.

Prendergast landed in waist-deep water just offshore. He released his parachute, inflated the bright yellow life-preserver around his waist and fired all the tracer bullets from his 0.38-cal pistol into the air. A dozen soldiers waded out to him, and since their guns were pointed in his direction, Prendergast raised his hands in surrender. One soldier saw his Navy issue revolver and took it. They began a slow, sloshy march toward

Lt(jg) Frank Prendergast prepares to man-up for a mission from *Kitty Hawk*. He hid a small pistol within his survival vest, which is seen here behind his oxygen mask. This photograph was taken weeks before the mission on which 'Flint River 605' (BuNo 151627) was shot down near Long Chau, northwest of Thanh Hoa. Prendergast managed to escape from militiamen who were in the water with him by shooting one of them with the previously concealed pistol (*Wattay*)

the shore, with Prendergast making the walk even slower by limping and acting dazed as to direction. First, the escorting VF-213 'Black Lions' Phantom II made passes, and even fired Sparrow air-to-air missiles at the beach. When two prowling A-1 Skyraiders from USS *Ticonderoga* (CVA-14) began strafing with their 20 mm cannon, most of the soldiers fled to the beach, leaving only their leader and one other with Prendergast.

Each time the aeroplanes came over, the North Vietnamese soldier armed with an AK-47 assault rifle would duck under water out of fear of being hit. Prendergast saw the SH-3 rescue helicopter from HS-8 approaching and decided it was then or never. The next time the soldier ducked, Prendergast pulled out a small 0.25-cal automatic pistol he kept in his flight suit and aimed at his guard. The guard pointed Prendergast's own revolver at him and pulled the trigger. Prendergast had counted correctly – the revolver had been emptied shooting tracers. There was a click as the hammer fell on an empty chamber. Prendergast shot him between the eyes with the small automatic.

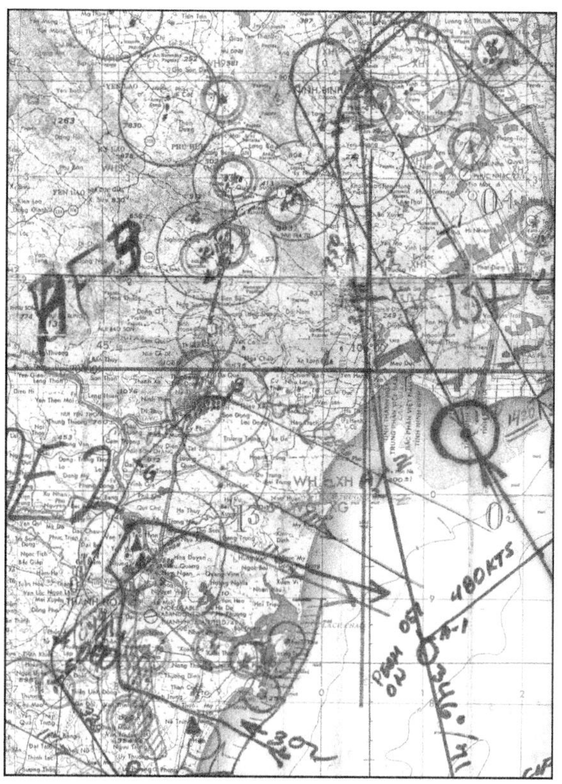

A section (which includes Thanh Hoa) of the chart used by Lt Cdr Al Wattay and Lt(jg) Frank Prendergast on six missions (note the different colours when the routes are close to each other) during RVAH-13's deployment on *Kitty Hawk* during 1966-67. Al Wattay was Frank Prendergast's usual pilot, but he was not with him the day he was shot down. Wattay's notes on the chart's symbols include large circles and partial circles in black lines for known SAM threat areas, and associated radar coverage. Black dots within the circles describe launching sites, while double green circles with stars denote heavy, long range AAA battery sites (maximum altitude of 37,000 ft). Green and red circles denote heavy and medium range AAA batteries, while solitary red circles mark out medium range AAA only. 'AE3' and 'AF2' were tactical package areas. Coloured lines denote individual mission profiles with headings and course lines. Finally, the blue circle with the dot was the point where Frank was shot down (*Wattay*)

When the second soldier came up from beneath the water, Prendergast hit him on the head, threw his AK-47 assault rifle in the water and headed for a nearby sand bar. The Vietnamese soldier picked up his gun and began to shoot. On the sandbar, Prendergast bought more time by stopping and raising his hands. As the helicopter came closer, he wheeled around, fired the pistol and ran. The SH-3 swooped broadside and the door gunner blasted the enemy soldier with a heavy M-61 machine gun. Prendergast jumped in and was flown back to *Kitty Hawk*. The Navy did not let him fly any more missions.

19 May was Ho Chi Minh's birthday, and in 1967 it became the worst single day for aircraft carriers on *Yankee Station* when six aircraft and ten aircrew were lost over North Vietnam. The missions flown that day saw naval aircraft attacking targets in Hanoi for the first time. Because of previous bombing restrictions, the defenders had had time to ring the capital with myriad AAA and SAM sites.

Inspired by Ho Chi Minh's birthday, the defenders downed two F-8s (and an A-4 the day before) from USS *Bon Homme Richard* (CVA-31), which was an *Essex* class carrier that did not operate RA-5Cs, an F-4 and an A-6 (and an A-4 the day before) from *Enterprise*, with RVAH-7 on board, and another Phantom II and a Vigilante from *Kitty Hawk*.

Assigned to RVAH-13, the RA-5C (BuNo 150826) from CVA-63 was on a mission to get BDA following the attack on the Van Dien military vehicle and SAM support depot near Hanoi, where the F-4 and A-6 from CVAN-65 had been shot down that morning. The jet was hit on its initial turn over Hanoi at 3500 ft and 700 knots, and it continued northwest in flames for ten miles before Lt Cdr James Griffin and Lt Jack Waiters ejected. Both men were captured and died in captivity.

An indication of the overall aggressiveness of CVW-11 aboard CVA-63, and the intensity of its early *Rolling Thunder* missions, was provided by the statistic that RVAH-13 lost more Vigilantes in two deployments than any other RVAH squadron during the entire war. Lt Cdrs Ray Vehorn and Dick Daum were the only airmen from the unit to survive both cruises.

Constellation returned for its third combat tour in May 1967, with RVAH-12 replacing RVAH-6 in CVW-14. The 'Speartips' of RVAH-12 were a new squadron that had completed a Mediterranean cruise with new RA-5Cs aboard *Saratoga* in 1966.

Vigilantes were not the only ones at risk during reconnaissance missions. Assigned to get coverage of the main Hanoi-Haiphong highway on 29 June 1967, the 'Speartip' RA-5C's escort was hit by groundfire. Despite battle-damage, VF-142 F-4B Phantom II 'Dakota 207' (BuNo 150439) made it all the way back to *Constellation* before its hydraulic fluid leaked away, the controls froze and the crew ejected.

BuNo 156632 of RVAH-3 formates with one of the TA-4s assigned to the 'Recce RAG' for pilot training, along with TA-3s. This photograph was taken over the Gulf of Mexico near the 'Vigi' community's last home at NAS Key West, in Florida. This Vigilante is now on display at Sanford Airport (*EBAL*)

One of RVAH-11's Vigilantes is barged off *Forrestal* following the devastating fire of 29 July 1967 which destroyed three RA-5Cs (*EBAL*)

Weary sailors look on as RA-5C BuNo 149284 is pushed over the side by *Forrestal's* 'Tilly' deck crane in the wake of the fire (*Mersky*)

RVAH-12's RA-5C BuNo 151727 was photographed just weeks prior to embarking in *Constellation* in April 1967 and heading off to war for the first time. Having survived two combat tours with the unit, this aircraft was stricken at Rota, Spain, in late January 1972 possibly after a heavy landing aboard *Independence* (*Mersky*)

Commanding RVAH-12 was Cdr Pat O'Gara, who revised reconnaissance tactics and was influential in the Vigilante community. After a tour on the CRAW-1 staff, he became the CO of the RAG, where he directed the training of all reconnaissance crews.

While in command of the Vigilante RAG, and later as ComReconWingOne (the top man in the Vigi community), O'Gara began a crusade to abolish the term 'heavy' left over from A-3 Skywarrior days – e.g. VAH-10 was called 'Heavy Ten'. At meetings, O'Gara would go to the board, scrawl RVAH in large letters and cross off the A and H as obsolete. Vigilante veterans identify when they joined the community by whether they say 'Heavy' or 'Recce' Three.

A month later RVAH-11, which had recently transitioned from A-3 Skywarriors, arrived in the Tonkin Gulf aboard the Atlantic Fleet carrier USS *Forrestal* (CVA-59). After only five days of operations, tragedy struck when a Zuni rocket fired from an F-4 struck the fuel tank of a Skyhawk which blew up, setting off a series of explosions and fires which ultimately killed 134 men and completely destroyed 21 aircraft. Three of these were RVAH-11's RA-5Cs BuNos 148932, 149284 and 149305.

After temporary repairs in the Philippines, *Forrestal* sailed back to Norfolk in September. The disaster threw schedules out of whack. Since the squadron was ready for combat, the RA-5Cs were replaced and RVAH-11 was back on the line by early December, this time with CVW-11 aboard *Kitty Hawk*.

From the time of the *Forrestal* fire at the end of July until RVAH-6 arrived in-theatre aboard *Ranger* in early November, the Navy's reconnaissance assets in the Tonkin Gulf comprised small detachments of RF-8 Crusaders on *Coral Sea*, *Oriskany* and *Intrepid*, and the Vigilantes of RVAH-12 on *Constellation*.

The 'Speartips' lost two jets and their crews in August. On the 13th, BuNo 151634 was hit by AAA while doing 720 knots on a mission near Lang Son, in the extreme northeast of North Vietnam. The Vigilante was enveloped in flame and the tail section came apart. Both crewmen were captured as soon as they touched down in their parachutes. Lt Cdr Leo Hyatt and Lt(jg) Wayne Goodermote, who were on their 33rd mission, were finally released, together, in 1973.

The end result of Vigilante reconnaissance. This photograph shows a North Vietnamese SAM site which was highlighted by the photo-interpreter who found it on the negative film after it was processed. Positive prints such as this were made for briefing flight crews and battle staffs (*Wattay*)

Four days later Vigilante BuNo 149302 crashed into the sea while on a coastal reconnaissance mission, killing squadron Executive Officer Cdr Laurent Dion and his RAN, Lt(jg) Charles Horn. There were insufficient facts to determine the exact cause, but the crash may have been another case of unnoticed small arms fire while on a mission.

August 1967 could have been named 'Month of the SAM', for 16 Navy aircraft were shot down, six of them by missiles. Pilot reports showed 249 SA-2 launches during the month, including 80 on 21 August. And the defences kept building. By late 1967, Hanoi was defended by 15 SAM sites, 560 AAA pieces of all calibres and MiG fighters at the nearby airfields of Gia Lam and Phuc Yen. The vital port city of Haiphong was similarly well protected. This was the welcome RVAH-6, -11 and -1 faced when they began their second combat tours.

The first Corsair IIs to see combat deployed aboard *Ranger* with RVAH-6 in 1967, and like the Intruders that first went to sea with RVAH-1 on *Independence*, they needed the Vigilante's SLR imagery to plan their strikes.

RAN Lt John Calhoun and Cdr C C Smith, the commanding officer of RVAH-6, flew 75 missions together over North Vietnam. One of their most significant took place on 16 December 1967, when their photographs revealed the exact location of the infamous 'Hanoi Hilton' prison camp in downtown Hanoi. Carol C Smith later became an admiral, and he held one of the top aviator jobs in the Navy as Commander Naval Air Forces Atlantic (CNAL).

SUPERMEN

By this time the Vigilante had established a fearsome reputation among pilots. Indeed, there were cases of officers turning down orders to an RVAH squadron out of fear of the aeroplane. The reputation was not completely undeserved, but came mostly from its early days in fleet service. The wing trailing- and leading-edge flaps were at 40 degrees for landing, and the trailing-edge flaps were the only section of the wing with Boundary Layer Control (BLC). This meant higher approach speeds with poor pitch response, and resulted in broken nose gears, flattened main-mount tyres and the occasional catastrophic ramp strike.

Starting with the A-5B, the trailing flap area was increased, leading- and trailing-edge flaps went to a 50-degree extension and the BLC moved to the leading-edge flaps (droops). The accident rate dropped, but if either of the two critical bulkheads cracked, what would have been a hard landing in another aeroplane turned into a major accident (Class A) because of the time and effort required to repair the damage. The 556 bulkhead had the main landing gear and forward engine mounts attached to it – the 556 was duly reinforced. The 742 bulkhead, mounting the horizontal slabs, vertical stabiliser and rear engine mounts, posed more of a problem.

A Vigilante 'in the groove', with hook down and flaps fully extended. Note the amount of black smoke coming from the J79 engines (the Phantom II suffered from the same problem). The smoke went away once afterburner (AB) was selected, so 'Vigi' crews always flew in AB when over the beach whether the speed was needed or not. Even with the RA-5C in minimum afterburner, escorting F-4s had trouble keeping up with the jet (*EBAL*)

Psychology also played a part as well. From the author's personal experience, when the answer to the question of what aeroplane he flew evoked the response 'Oh wow, aren't Vigilantes awfully difficult to fly, especially landing on the ship?', a natural reaction was to stand a little straighter and say, 'Yes, but I can hack it'! Thus, the unspoken implication was that the pilot was some sort of superman.

The author flew the RA-5C for seven years, and for part of this time he was the RVAH-3 LSO. His views on landing the Vigilante are as follows;

An unidentified Vigilante closes on the flight deck under the watchful gaze of the LSOs, who are in radio contact with the pilot. A plane guard UH-2 hovers in the background (*Mersky*)

'Landing any aeroplane on a ship is a challenge – doubly so at night. Yet, despite its fearsome reputation, the RA-5C did well day and night. Many RVAH squadrons and individual Vigilante pilots won air wing landing competitions. Training was the key. Not only for the pilots, but the LSOs. Waving the "heavies" – A-5s and A-3s – was a special skill. LSOs from those communities had no trouble with each others jets, but the LSOs from units equipped with "little" aeroplanes were intimidated, and did not always appreciate the effects of mass and inertia.

'I always felt the hardest thing to do in a "Vigi" was not land on the boat, but get in position for the catapult shot. The RA-5C used a bridle attached to two hooks under the intakes to launch, rather than the current nose-launch bar. This meant the nose wheel had to go up and over the catapult shuttle, but not too far. The shuttle was shaped like a turtle shell with the end chopped off, and it was slippery with an amalgam of jet fuel, condensed steam and salt spray. From the deck, the Vigilante had to be turned precisely on the centre of the cat track. Because of the length of the fuselage, there was little distance to correct the line-up. At the shuttle, the tolerances became even closer. If not aligned with the exact centre of the hump, the nose gear would slip off the edge and cut the tyre. You would add power to get over the hump, feel the wheel drop, and if you did not stop within two inches, you would crack the hold-back fitting in the tail.

'A good taxi director would modify the standard signals and add lots of body english. He would vary the speed and distance of his waving

An RVAH-1 RA-5C commences its catapult shot from bow cat one aboard *Ranger* in 1970. Most 'Vigi' pilots found that correctly positioning the jet over the catapult shuttle for launch was more difficult than landing back aboard the ship (*Mersky*)

Alone on the deck of *Kitty Hawk*, this RVAH-6 Vigilante gives an impression of the overall size of the jet. A large aeroplane to be on an aircraft carrier, it stretched 76.5 ft from its slender nose probe to the tip of the tail. Its wingspan was some 56 ft. To save space, NAA had the Vigilante fold on four sides – the wing tips folded up (as shown), the radome folded up and took the pitot-static probe with it, and the top of the vertical tail could fold to one side. Following its retirement in the late 1970s, this aeroplane (BuNo 156632) was all set to become a target at China Lake until it was rescued, restored and eventually put on display at Sanford airport, in Florida (*EBAL*)

hands. His body would lean and twist, shoulders dip and head nod with subtle signals to the pilot. He could have become a ballet dancer or professional mime with the skills needed to launch an RA-5C.'

1968

The nature of the air war over North Vietnam changed with a flip of the calendar. Weather was a factor as the Northeast Monsoon swept in, making visual bombing impossible for most of the first three months of 1968. The Intruders, using their all-weather navigation and attack systems – and radar imagery from the Vigilante's SLR – flew single aircraft strikes into North Vietnam no matter what the time of day, or the weather. Four of the solitary Intruders were lost in 90 days.

On 23 January, the American surveillance ship USS *Pueblo* (AGER-2) was surrounded by North Korean patrol boats and forced to surrender. *Enterprise* with RVAH-1 embarked, was in Sasebo, Japan, at the time, and it immediately set sail into the Sea of Japan. *Ranger* and RVAH-6 left *Yankee Station* on 27 January and arrived off the Korean coast on 1 February. A number of 'photo recce' missions were flown while both carriers sailed in Korean waters for a month. The sole 'big deck' carrier in the Tonkin Gulf at this time was *Kitty Hawk*, whose RVAH-11 and the rest of CVW-11 spent a record 61 days on the line.

Soon after leaving Korean waters, RVAH-6 became the first squadron to get the new AAS-21 IR mapping system fitted into its jets. RA-5Cs were flown to NAF Atsugi for installation of the new equipment, which would eventually be seen in all Vigilantes. The IR mapper was a major improvement in the jet's night capability, for no longer would the hazardous flashers be the only way to obtain imagery. The system used liquid nitrogen to cool sensing crystals which detected temperature differences. The AAS-21 could show dead vegetation used as camouflage, detect the hot engines of vehicles in the night and even show patterns of warmth where vehicles or aeroplanes had been parked.

In an amusing incident, early runs with the AAS-21 over the Ho Chi Minh Trail showed hot spots that IO and PIs could not figure out. The hot spots turned out to be fresh elephant droppings.

Back in Albany, Georgia, while the system was still classified as secret, an unmarked Beech 18 arrived at the naval air station and was kitted out

KA-3B BuNo 138959 of VAH-4 Det 63 passes fuel to an RA-5C of RVAH-11 after the latter had completed a photo-reconnaissance mission over North Vietnam in January 1968 (*Mersky*)

with the AAS-21 system. It duly flew a series of night flights, fuelling speculation on base as to what it was up to. The 'twin' Beech was being operated by the US Alcohol and Firearms Bureau in an effort to locate illicit whiskey stills in the hills of northern Georgia. Later, the 'Vigis' themselves would fly these 'revenoo-er' searches.

An IR image of the port most frequently used by Navy aircraft carriers during the Vietnam War. To the right of the photograph is the naval base at Subic Bay and across the river, the city of Olongapo. NAS Cubi Point, with its single runway and carrier pier, is across the bay from the naval base. The slight distortion present in this image comes from the line-scan that the AAS-21 used to register temperature differentials (*EBAL*)

From *Yankee Station*, RVAH-6 performed a series of runs at twilight, and an altitude of just 1500 ft, south to north along the coast of North Vietnam from the demilitarised zone to Haiphong. Using SLR, the jets were looking for 'Styx' anti-ship missiles and patrol boats prior to the battleship USS *Missouri* (BB-63) entering coastal waters and shelling the Thanh Hoa bridge.

RVAH-6 CO Cdr C C Smith made the first run, and XO Cdr Ivan Lewis the next. They were both shot at by heavy 85 mm anti-aircraft guns. Lt Cdr Herm Mueller and his RAN, Lt Guthrie, flew the third mission in an exact repeat of the first two. Abeam Vinh, Mueller avoided a pair of SAMs. A third came at him while he was steeply banked and low, and knowing that SA-2s always came in twos, he pushed forward on the stick and the fourth missile barely went over the Vigilante. Flak was heavy all through his manoeuvring. Shaken, he aborted the remainder of the run and headed back to *Ranger*.

The Bob Hope USO troupe with songstress Barbara McNair was on board for a show that night, and when she heard of the hazardous near miss, the singer ventured down to the LSO platform and Larry DeBoxtel handed her the radio. When Mueller called, '"Field Goal 603", Vigilante, Ball', McNair replied, 'C'mon home, baby. We're waiting for you'!

Lt Cdr DeBoxtel was assigned the fourth try. 'Box' had chosen 'Tiny' Mulholland as his RAN when they were in training, 'Because he was a great big guy, and would be useful if we ever jumped out'. Mulholland said there was no way he was going if they repeated the previous flight path, so they pretended to be a Shrike missile-carrying A-4 looking for SAM radars. They stayed high and flew in figure-eights just off Haiphong Harbour. The fire-control radars would lock-on when they headed away and shut down when they headed in. After several patterns, Mulholland turned off the jet's IFF transponder and DeBoxtel put the RA-5C into a supersonic dive down to 1500 ft, headed south. They got the coverage and the Vigilante was not fired at.

One week after the *Pueblo* capture, the Tet Offensive began. The Navy carriers remaining in the Gulf shifted to operations in South Vietnam in support of the Army and Marines. This discouraging show of strength by the North Vietnamese and Viet Cong moved President Johnson to try new initiatives to end the war. On 31 March he declared an end to attacks north of the 19th parallel. This meant Thanh Hoa and the infamous 'Iron Triangle' – Nam Dinh-Haiphong-Hanoi – was off-limits. The day was

1 April in Vietnam, and many thought the message was an April Fool's joke. The reaction of flight crews was mixed. On the one hand, they were no longer exposing themselves to the heaviest air defences in history, but they also knew that the North Vietnamese would use the break – as they had done on earlier, shorter bombing pauses – to re-equip and rearm. They correctly felt that if they could have kept up the pressure of 1967, the communist leaders in Hanoi would have quit.

Peace talks in Paris began in May with quibbles about the shape of the table(!), and then proceeded to drag on with more trivial arguments. Navy aircraft flew missions into the narrow panhandle of North Vietnam and increasingly into Laos and Cambodia in an attempt to stop the flow of enemy supplies into South Vietnam.

Vinh, and the area surrounding the city, remained hot as the North Vietnamese shifted defences from the 'Iron Triangle'. CVW-9 CO Cdr Paul Peck aboard *Enterprise* used the intelligence RVAH-1 brought back to good effect. IR imagery had picked up a great deal of truck traffic around the old cathedral in Vinh. This was suspicious, and a 'Smoking Tiger' RA-5C made a surprise, fast, low photo pass at dawn. The processed film showed a missile transporter backed up to the nave, loading SA-2s into the cathedral. CAG Peck grabbed the photograph while it was still wet and ran with it to the admiral.

During the ensuing mini-alpha strike, the first bomb caused a secondary explosion that went up to 8000 ft. Flaming, falling debris ignited nearby buildings, which also exploded.

On 5 May, 'Comanche Trail 102' (BuNo 149278) of RVAH-1 was photographing Route 1A from 6500 ft near Ha Tinh when, as the escort described it, 'The "Vigi" burst into a huge fireball about twice the size of the aircraft and snap-rolled when the starboard wing came off'. Lts Giles Norrington and Lt Dick Tangeman somehow managed to eject, although they were injured in the process and soon captured. They had crewed together since converting onto the RA-5C in 1965, and had flown 22 combat missions. Both men were released in March 1973.

Cdr Charlie James, the executive officer of RVAH-11, was a veteran of the Korean War, where he had flown AD Skyraiders with VA-55. On 18 May, James was flying 'Glen Rock 606' (BuNo 149283) northwest of Vinh, close to the western border of the panhandle, when the jet was hit by a 57 mm burst – even 10,000 ft was not high enough to avoid larger calibre AAA. The jet burst into flames and broke up, forcing James and his RAN, Lt Cdr Vincent Monroe, to eject. Two rescue beepers were heard and SAR aircraft headed for the area, but there was too much AAA to continue the rescue attempt. Radio Hanoi reported the capture of the crew, and although James was released in 1973, Monroe died in captivity.

After losing eight aircraft in combat and another seven in accidents during its 125 days on-the-line, *Kitty Hawk* finished its third war cruise in June and returned home.

Between the March partial halt and the full suspension in November, the Navy lost seven A-4s, ten A-7s, eight F-4s, six A-6s and two RA-5Cs to enemy action. In November, all of North Vietnam was declared free from attack. The air war had entered a new phase. The days of the massive Alpha strikes were over. Reconnaissance missions over the North would continue, however.

FROM HIGHWAY PATROL TO PROTECTIVE REACTION

After the United States decreed a bombing halt, the crews flying off the carriers spent so much time over the Ho Chi Minh Trail in Laos that they mockingly called themselves the 'Laotian Highway Patrol'. They even wore an embroidered shoulder patch modelled after a real police badge. While the air war was not the brawl of 1967, the AAA threat was always there. The enemy was capable of surprises, and airmen could not let themselves become complacent. For the attack units the emphasis changed from strikes to close air support and the *Commando Hunt* interdiction campaign. Destroying supplies moving south was difficult, and routes required frequent reconnaissance.

The image of the Ho Chi Minh Trail as some sort of highway is incorrect. Very little was paved, the Trail being a series of parallel dirt roads, jungle trails and footpaths which were interconnected. When one section was blocked, traffic shunted to another. Stopping the flow was an impossible task, but the US Navy and Air Force tried. While the reconnaissance squadrons were a part of the 'Laotian Highway Patrol', they also continued to fly over North Vietnam with good reason.

ARF

The air-refuelling probe on a Vigilante retracted to streamline the aeroplane for high speed. When the switch was flipped, doors popped open and an obscenely red, bent pipe with a grey tip came out of the left side of the nose. Wind across the probe, and its doors, made a racket.

For most missions over Vietnam, the Vigilante carried sufficient internal fuel – twice as much as its usual escort, the F-4. Also, for combat, the Phantom II had AIM-9 Sidewinder missiles on pylons below the wings, a huge fuel tank hung on the belly and AIM-7

An extended air refuelling probe. The open doors made so much noise in the air stream that it could be heard in the cockpit (*Woodul*)

Sparrow missiles protruding from the fuselage. Although the two jets had the same J79 engines, the RA-5C could outrun its fighter escort because the jet carried no external stores, and was 'clean' aerodynamically.

Vigilante pilots did practise refuelling for the times ARF (Airborne Re-Fuelling) would be necessary. A favourite pastime was to do two 'dry plugs', retract the probe, pull alongside the tanker to show you were clear, then light the burners and pull away in a swooping barrel-roll while your escort was lazing alongside the tanker, conserving every bit of fuel.

Aerial refuelling in a Vigilante was difficult. The pitching moment arm was long, and an up or down correction resulted in the probe twisting in an arc. Just before contact, airflow over the nose shoved the basket off to the side. The secret was to aim halfway out at the drogue's 'ten o'clock'. KA-3 'Whales' and KA-6s were the favourites for ARF. Their drogue-baskets were larger than those on the D-404 buddy store, and they had lots of fuel 'give away'. Bomber A-6s and the small A-4 Skyhawk became temporary tankers by hanging a self-contained buddy store on the centreline pylon, but their baskets were small and they did not have much 'give'. The use of A-7s as tankers made ARF more awkward for 'Vigis' and Crusaders, which had fuel probes on the left. Since the Corsair II had no centreline station, the Phantom IIs and other A-7s with probes on the right side dictated the buddy store be hung on the left. This meant the RA-5C had to fight the turbulence from the tanker's jet exhaust.

'Join the Navy and See the World' was the recruiting slogan and the Norfolk, Virginia, based aircraft carrier USS *America* (CVA-66) delivered. On the first of its three deployments to Vietnam, the ship with and its air wing went around the world. In 1968, the 'Bats' of RVAH-13 got to visit Rio de Janeiro and cross the South Atlantic and Indian Oceans (a visit to South Africa was cancelled for political reasons) on the way to its third combat deployment. The air war was still hot – bombing restriction and the full pause were months away – when RVAH-13 arrived on the line, but it did not lose a single RA-5C, compared to the five lost in 1966 and 1967. The unit had the dubious distinction of losing more jets in combat than any other RVAH squadron.

At the end of the cruise, the decision was made to fly all the RVAH-13 RA-5Cs home, rather than wait while CVA-66 sailed halfway round the world. KA-3Bs were the tankers for the long flight. Lt Cdr Bob 'Kid' Kuhlke had a hydraulic failure on Johnston Island;

'Johnston Island is in the middle of nowhere, and they sure didn't have a lot of facilities to fix a broken "Vigi". The local engineers jury-rigged a wobble pump to re-do my hydraulic system. I think they were happy about a change of routine. The pump was a real contraption, but it worked. I caught up with the unit in Hawaii. Whole trip took a week.'

Constellation now had RVAH-5 on board, and the carrier arrived in *WestPac* in time to adjust to the new operational restrictions. Up to January 1969, all reconnaissance flights over North Vietnam had been coded UE *Blue Tree* missions, but they were rarely differentiated from the overall *Rolling Thunder* bombing campaign. This changed after the bombing halt was declared. From 1 November 1968, reconnaissance flights became the main reason for sending jets into North Vietnam. A 'Savage Son' RA-5C was the first Navy reconnaissance aircraft lost on a *Blue Tree* mission after the halt.

The flight crews of RVAH-5 pose for a cruise book shot. The variety of hats is typical. Bush hats, Marine fatigue caps, baseball caps and even regulation uniform hats took turns in the fashion parade. Eleven crewmembers for a deployed RVAH unit was typical, making up five crews and one extra. Crew strength was matched to the number of aeroplanes assigned, and logically grew smaller as the RVAHs shrunk in size from six to five to four Vigilantes (*Powell*)

On 25 November 1968, radar-guided anti-aircraft guns tracked 'Old Kentucky 113' (BuNo 149293) two miles northwest of Vinh as the pilot, Cdr Ernest Stamm, jinked wildly at 550 knots in an attempt to throw off the gunners' aim. His manoeuvring was to no avail. The jet was hit and exploded into four parts. The escorting Phantom IIs had heard the tones of a 'Fan Song' SAM radar on their ALQ gear, so it was uncertain whether flak or an SA-2 had destroyed the RA-5C. Two parachutes were seen, but neither Cdr Stamm or RAN, Lt(jg) Richard Thurn, survived.

An RVAH-5 Vigilante launches off the bow catapult of *Constellation* in 1968 in the Tonkin Gulf. On 25 November that same year this aircraft, BuNo 149293, was shot down by radar-guided AAA two miles northwest of Vinh. The jet exploded into four parts, and neither the pilot, Cdr Ernest Stamm, or RAN, Lt(jg) Richard Thurn, survived (*EBAL*)

TORA, TORA, TORA

On 6 January 1969, *Enterprise* left Alameda, California, with CVW-9 and RVAH-6 on board. As usual for Pacific Fleet carriers, the ship and air wing would train around the Hawaiian Islands until the culminating Operational Readiness Inspection (ORI), after which it would depart for the war zone. The first morning out of Pearl Harbor, hot exhaust from a jet-starter cooked off a missile and started a conflagration on the flight deck. The fire and explosions killed 27 men and destroyed 15 aeroplanes. The reason relatively few sailors were killed was that all hands were standing by at General Quarters (GQ) stations as part of the training exercise. At GQ, ship's compartments are isolated, firefighting and damage control parties are manned and their equipment is ready.

Besides the destruction from actual explosions and fire, many aeroplanes were badly affected by the salt water used to fight the fire. Some had to have holes punched in them to drain the water out. All were washed down with fresh water as soon as possible. One RVAH-6 jet was damaged by shrapnel, but it was repaired and flew again within four days. Ironically, this jet (BuNo 150842) would be shot down two months later.

Those aircraft that were either repairable or undamaged were craned onto barges and taken to NAS Barbers Point, on Oahu. Air wing training resumed while CVAN-65 was being repaired in Pearl Harbor, although the sortie schedule was relaxed, with flying only from Monday through to Friday. The 'Fleurs' of RVAH-6 mapped the entire Hawaiian Island chain, and used their unique IR sensors to locate a steam leak in downtown Honolulu. Announcements were made on radio and television to inform the public about what the low-flying Vigilantes were up to.

Sharing the airfield at the time were the replica Aichi 'Vals' and Mitsubishi Zeros (made-up from AT-6 Texans and Vultee BT-13 trainers in the best Hollywood tradition) used during the filming of the motion picture *Tora, Tora, Tora*, which retold the story of the 1941 attack on Pearl Harbor. The 'Fleurs', with their photographic capability, took many stills of the mock Japanese aeroplanes.

After six weeks ashore, five days completing the ORI and the voyage across the Pacific, RVAH-6 was back in the Tonkin Gulf on 31 March.

On the first launch of the first day back on the line, a Vigilante had mechanical problems and did not launch. RA-5C BuNo 150842 on the next launch, piloted by Cdr Dan White, the squadron maintenance officer, with RAN Lt Ramey Carpenter, catapulted off but did not return.

'Field Goal 601' and its Phantom II escort were flying northeast of Nakhon Phanom, in Laos, and the RA-5C was in a steep turn at 5000 ft and 420 knots when it burst into flames and fell apart – the large centre section went into a flat spin. There were no ejections. The escort did not see any gunfire before the Vigilante exploded, but it was fired on immediately afterwards. The remains of the crew were recovered and identified in 1997. Since there were official doubts that the jet was a combat loss, a detailed accident investigation was conducted. Lt Cdr Larry DeBoxtel had just become the new Safety Officer for RVAH-6;

'The skipper ran us through a crash drill, all the reports and paperwork, on the way back from Hawaii . When White went down,

RVAH-6's BuNo 151617 was photographed during *Enterprise's* 1969 *WestPac*. A deck crewmember gives the pilot a thumbs up, while others stand by the main wheels with chocks in case of brake failure. The chocks would hopefully hold the aeroplane still long enough for deck crews to secure the RA-5C with tie-down chains. This was a standard practice on all aircraft carriers. BuNo 151617 survived frontline service to be stricken at NAS Key West in November 1976 (*Wells*)

One of the first nine production A3J-1s to leave NAA in late 1959, this aircraft initially spent time with the Naval Air Test Center at NAS Patuxent River conducting ECM trials. Converted into an RA-5C, it eventually served with RVAH-6 in the late 1960s. Seen here flying over San Francisco during CVW-9 work-ups, it deployed with *Enterprise* on *WestPac* in early January 1969. Stricken from Navy service in 1975 and placed on display at NAS Lakehurst in 1982, the aircraft was destroyed some years later when it was in transit from Lakehurst to its new home at the Victory Air Museum in New Jersey (*Mersky*)

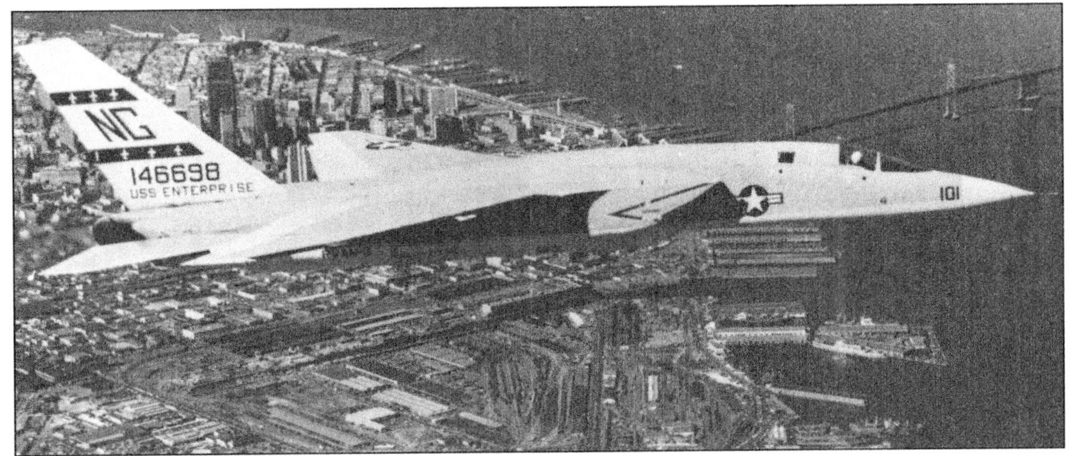

The CO of RVAH-6, Cdr Ed Feeks congratulates Lt Cdr Al Best (on the ladder) after the unit's final flight of the 1969 *WestPac* deployment on *Enterprise* as part of CVW-9. On 16 June 1969, BuNo 150841 (seen here) flew three missions and passed 2000 hours flight time since its acceptance by the Navy – the first Vigilante to do so. The black-edged rectangle forward of the ladder was where the maintenance chief wrote the aircraft's weight for the catapult crew to compute their settings (*Wells*)

all I had to do was change names and numbers on the reports. We came up with some speculation on the cause – fuel tank explosion, overstress – but I'm convinced it was AAA. They were on a second run over the target'.

The deployment was disrupted again when the North Koreans shot down an unarmed US Navy EC-121 surveillance aircraft on 15 April 1969, and RVAH-6 was sent to the Sea of Japan for a second crisis. RVAH-9 aboard *Ranger* (the carrier the 'Fleurs' had been on during the *Pueblo* crisis) joined them. The 'Hooters' had been successfully operating off Vietnam since the end of November.

When the crisis over the downing of the EC-121 subsided *Ranger* headed home, transferring one of its Vigilantes to RVAH-6 to replace the jet lost over Laos. In the Tonkin Gulf, meanwhile, RVAH-11 and CVA-63 again played a lone hand, being extended at sea.

While the period off Korea began badly due to maintenance problems, RVAH-6 recovered and gathered valuable intelligence, before returning to Vietnam for a short second, and last line, period. Six Vigilantes were assigned to the unit, but the ship allowed only four to be on board, and one of these had to be struck down in the hangar deck. This was an early indication of the size reduction RVAH units would suffer in the future.

There were two reasons why five, then four and, towards the end, only three RA-5Cs were assigned to a squadron. The size of the aeroplane (76 ft long and a 53-ft wingspan) made the Vigilante unpopular on carrier flight decks, where space was at a premium. Additionally, many types of maintenance required that the internal fuel cans be removed. Because the latter were designed as part of the A-5 weapons delivery system, they were mounted on rails so that they could slide out when released (the mechanics had a 'creeper' on wheels they could roll back and forth while working). Although easy to do on land, such a system was impractical on a ship, where the jet had to have its tail, plus the length of the can and space to work, over the deck.

Since most carrier-based aircraft are parked with their aft ends sticking out over the water and their main wheels at the edge of the deck, removing the cans from a Vigilante took over a large piece of flight deck real estate.

The second reason was a lack of RA-5Cs. CRAW-1 constantly had to swap aeroplanes among the squadrons in an effort to balance deployment needs, maintenance and overhaul requirements. Since the jet had proven itself a valuable asset as the war in South-east Asia expanded, NAA built 36 new RA-5Cs at its Columbus plant. Even these were not enough to meet all the requirements, and every 'Vigi' lost in combat, or otherwise, made the situation more difficult.

After *Enterprise* returned to *Yankee Station*, Lt Cdr DeBoxtel had a misadventure. He recalls;

'The ship left, and "Tiny" (Lt Wayne Mulholland) and I stayed in Cubi to fly one of our jets, which was having its engines changed. We went to the O-club on top of the hill and played bingo after dinner. Darned, if we didn't win a bottle of Chivas Regal – a gallon bottle! When the aeroplane was ready, we wrapped up the Scotch really well to take back to the ship. Illegal or not, no way we were leaving it behind.

Sometimes the Vigilante's unique linear bay fuel cans would come loose during a catapult shot, land on the flight deck and explode with spectacular results. In this sequence, all three tanks (and the 885 US gallons of fuel they contained) were lost from the RVAH-12 jet flown by Cdr John Huber when launching from *Independence* on 4 September 1969. Three cans are visible in the lower photo. The Vigilante usually remained flyable in the wake of such an incident (*EBAL*)

'On the way, "Tiny's" navigation system "dumped" and then our TACAN failed. Solid undercast below us. We started having oxygen problems, so I dropped through a hole in the cloud deck. We were over Hainan Island! Over the radio, I heard a broken call about MiGs launching. I looked and could see the silver shapes lifting off. I turned fast, lit the burners, pushed over and got to 1.3 mach on the way south. A couple of Navy F-4s from *Enterprise* passed us going the other way.

'Fortunately, other than a good scare, nothing came of it – unlike some of the other poor guys that flew over that Chinese island by mistake. And, yes, the Chivas tasted great.'

Life in the Vigilante squadrons did not always run smoothly. Units are, after all, not just aeroplanes, but people too. RVAH-7 had finished a deployment to the Mediterranean (losing BuNo 147854 along the way) and was on its turn-around cycle at NAS Albany when the XO tried to loop a Vigilante – a difficult manoeuvre, which required plenty of altitude and a supersonic entry speed. The Vigilante (BuNo 149287) departed controlled flight and the crew ejected. The errant executive officer was swiftly replaced.

Normally, a new Executive Officer would be found, but at the same time the commanding officer quit flying, citing severe personal problems. The unit also had other problems, and deployment on *Constellation* was less than two months away. Lt Cdr Art Skelly (of the inverted over Haiphong adventure) became the senior officer.

Cdr Bob Donaldson had recently returned from *WestPac*, where he had been the CO of RVAH-13 for the cruise on *America*. He had a reputation as a good leader, and the reconnaissance wing commodore (CRAW-1) drafted him to take over and straighten out RVAH-7. As a condition, Cdr Donaldson took along Lt Cdr Dan Rowley, who had been in A3Js, and was then a RAN instructor in RVAH-3. Their adventure began when all their gear could not be taken to San Diego in time. Once underway, and he had had a chance to learn who was doing what, Donaldson duly replaced the Maintenance Officer and the XO.

Lt Cdr Dan Rowley (left) and Lt Cdr Art Skelly served together in RVAH-7 in 1969-70 aboard *Constellation*. They had known each other prior to joining the unit, and would remain friends long after leaving it. Art Skelly had the unusual career pattern of flying helicopters and anti-submarine warfare aircraft before instructing in jets and finessing orders (his wife was a bridesmaid at the assignment officer's wedding!) to A-3s. He was in VAH-6 at NAS Whidbey along with Bob Davis, Jim Thompson, and Gary Getter. Skelly stayed in 'Six' for its transition to RA-5Cs, and made the 1966 cruise on *Constellation*, where he flew inverted over Haiphong, got shot up and had his RAN lose his canopy. He instructed in the 'Recce RAG' before the tour with RVAH-7. Another assignment to RVAH-3 followed, before Skelly became RVAH-7's XO and CO during *Kitty Hawk*'s 11-month deployment in 1972. Dan Rowley was one of the original Vigilante BNs to deploy in A3Js with VAH-7 on *Enterprise*. He transitioned with the 'Peacemakers' to the RA-5C, and stayed with them for the 1966 *WestPac* deployment. Pulled from instructing in the RAG, he went to RVAH-7 again. After that Rowley graduated from the Navy Test Pilot School at Patuxent River, and spent several years doing test work before becoming the XO and CO of RVAH-6 (*Rowley*)

In RVAH-7 at this time was a senior RAN, Lt 'P J', who rubbed many people the wrong way. The Premier of South Vietnam, the flamboyant Nguyen Cao Ky, was coming to CVA-64 on an official visit, and Lt 'P J' was proposed to be a tour escort. Lt(jg) Billy Beaver protested that 'P J' would not present the correct image of naval aviation, and Cdr Donaldson agreed, so Beaver got to show Cao Ky the Vigilante instead.

Late in the cruise, Cdr Donaldson left to become the CO of RVAH-3. A year after that, his replacement tried to take-off from NAS Albany in a Vigilante with the flaps up and he ejected when the aeroplane would not lift off properly. The crash crew reached into the canopy-less cockpit to shut down the engines. The Vigilante flew again, but the pilot did not. RVAH-7 went through another shuffle of commanders.

NEW DECADE

For RVAH-7, 1 January 1970 meant a tragic, non-combat loss. Traditionally, the commander of a Navy air wing flew all of the aircraft assigned, although by the Vietnam era, CAG was checked out in only two types from the ship. Cdr Randell K Billings, commander of CVW-14, had asked to fly a Vigilante while the ship was in port at Cubi Point for the holidays. Lt 'P J' was to be his backseater. Lt(jg) Beaver again thought 'P J' an inappropriate choice, and he complained to the CO. He was allowed to take the flight with CAG instead.

What went wrong will never be known, but the Vigilante (BuNo 148928) went into a steep dive with the engines at high thrust. Beaver tried frantically to talk to the pilot, and when there was no response, he ejected (the RA-5C did not have a system where the RAN could eject the pilot, but the pilot could eject the RAN). Unfortunately, they were going faster than Mach 1. Beaver's lower connection to his seat-pan was found unfastened – he had probably released it while trying to re-seat the communication leads. The high speed ejection with a loose seat-pan broke Billy Beaver's neck, tore apart the parachute canopy, and he was killed. The jet made such a deep hole that CAG's body was not recovered.

Although Lt Cdr Rowley was particularly upset because Beaver had been a student of his going through the RAG, it was Lt 'P J' who was chosen to escort the body home because 'he could be spared from combat operations'. Lt 'P J' decided since he was on the selection list for lieutenant commander, but had not yet been officially promoted, he would wear the insignia of the higher rank on the trip. On the helicopter flight back to CVA-64, he was seen pulling the gold oak leaves off his collar and putting the silver bars back.

If war can ever be said to be routine, the remainder of 1969 and all of 1970 were, at least for Navy airmen. Richard Nixon was the new

A 'Checkertail' RA-5C traps on *Kitty Hawk* in 1969. A stablemate (with the squadron emblem on its side) and two VF-213 F-4Bs are chained down on deck behind the recovering Vigilante. The 'Black Lions' of VF-213 undertook all six of its Vietnam combat deployments in *Kitty Hawk* with CVW-11, during which time it escorted Vigilantes from RVAH-6 (one cruise), RVAH-7 (one) RVAH-11 (two) and RVAH-13 (two) (*EBAL*)

American president, the first US troop reductions in South Vietnam had taken place and the peace talks in Paris dragged on. There was a brief flurry of strikes into North Vietnam in May 1970, but almost all other flights were over South Vietnam, Laos or Cambodia. RVAH-11, -7, -5 and -12 came and went, taking their turns running reconnaissance over the trail in Laos, gathering electronic data on PECM tracks and going north on rare *Blue Tree* missions.

Because of the demands of the war in Vietnam, in 1968 36 new Vigilantes were authorised. NAR (there had been a corporate buy-out) added the latest avionics, put in higher thrust J79-GE-10 engines and improved the airframe by redesigning the intakes and adding a fillet to the leading edge of the wing where it joined the fuselage. The result was much better handling at approach speeds. By all the designation rules, these jets should have been RA-5Ds. However, the politics of procurement and budget being what they are, the new batch remained RA-5Cs. Within the community, the new Vigilante's were referred to as '156 series' after their Navy bureau numbers. The last 156 Vigilantes (140 were new or rebuilt RA-5Cs) were delivered in August 1970, and later that year RVAH-1 and -6 became the first squadrons to take the new jets to *WestPac*.

In 1969 there was to be a London-New York Mail Race. The goal was to get a letter from a city post office in central London to a downtown post office in Manhattan. There were numerous classes, which included commercial passenger and light aeroplanes. A Vigilante was prepared to win the unlimited prize.

CRAW-1 Capt G W Kimmons and Lt Cdr Dave Turner went to Columbus to pick up a new 156 series Vigilante. Its reconnaissance canoe had not yet installed, and the jet's J79-GE-10 turbojets were 'race-tuned'. Its paint had also been carefully applied. NAR engineers said the usual mach two speed restriction was Navy conservatism, and the aeroplane was capable of higher speeds. On a practice run for the race at Albany, the Vigilante went to 2.5 mach, and the pilot, Lt Cdr Robert 'Beef' Renner, said he felt that the jet could go even faster. Dave Turner was a finalist for the racing RAN;

'We planned the race to the last ounce of gas, fractions of a minute. A series of KA-3 tankers over the Atlantic (*text continues on page 63*)

A 'Savage Sons' Vigilante is motioned onto *Ranger's* catapult. The taxi director has his hands raised, and steam from a previous launch is rising off the cat track. Later transferred to RVAH-7, this aircraft (BuNo 149287) was lost when the squadron XO attempted a loop at NAS Albany in 1969 (*EBAL*)

COLOUR PLATES

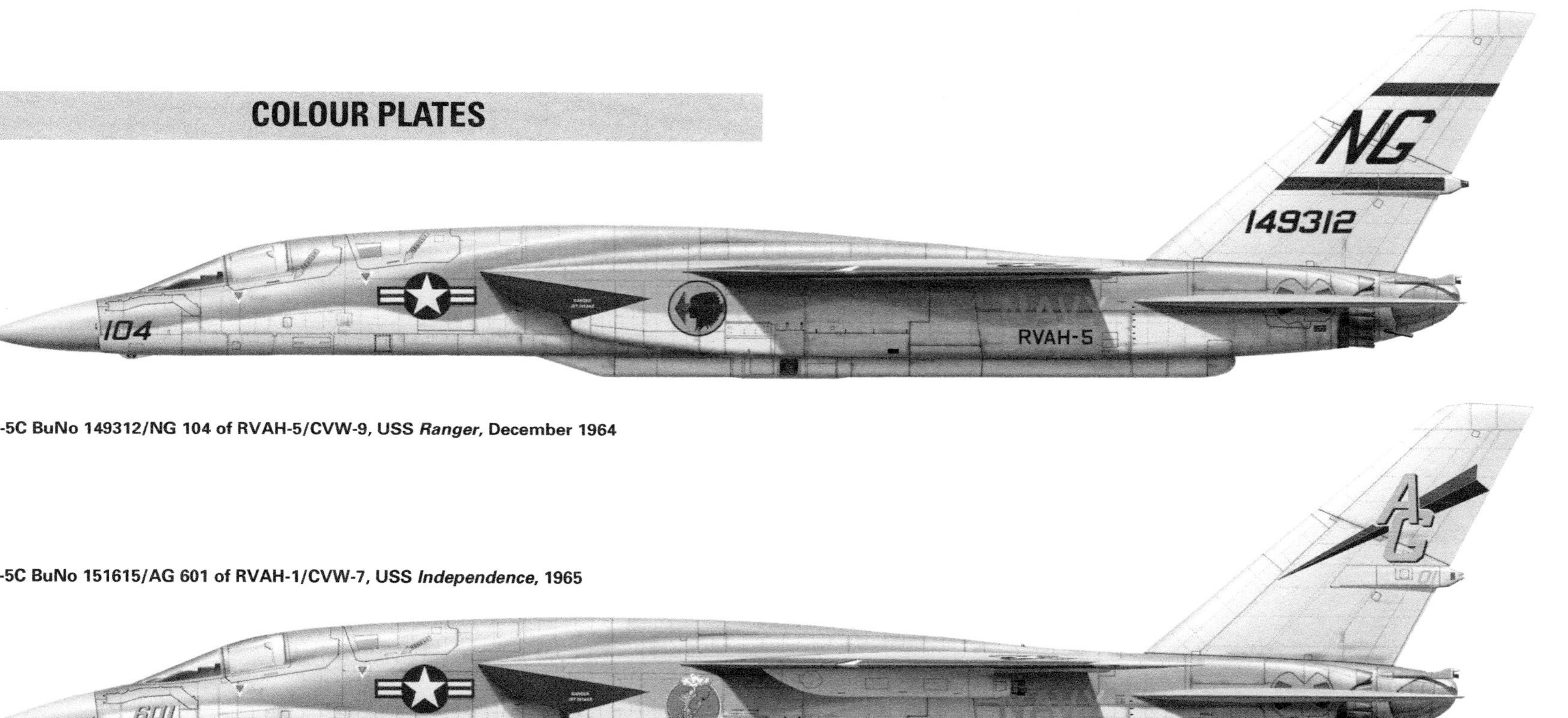

1
RA-5C BuNo 149312/NG 104 of RVAH-5/CVW-9, USS *Ranger*, December 1964

2
RA-5C BuNo 151615/AG 601 of RVAH-1/CVW-7, USS *Independence*, 1965

3
RA-5C BuNo 151633/NG 102 of RVAH-7/CVW-9, USS *Enterprise*, December 1965

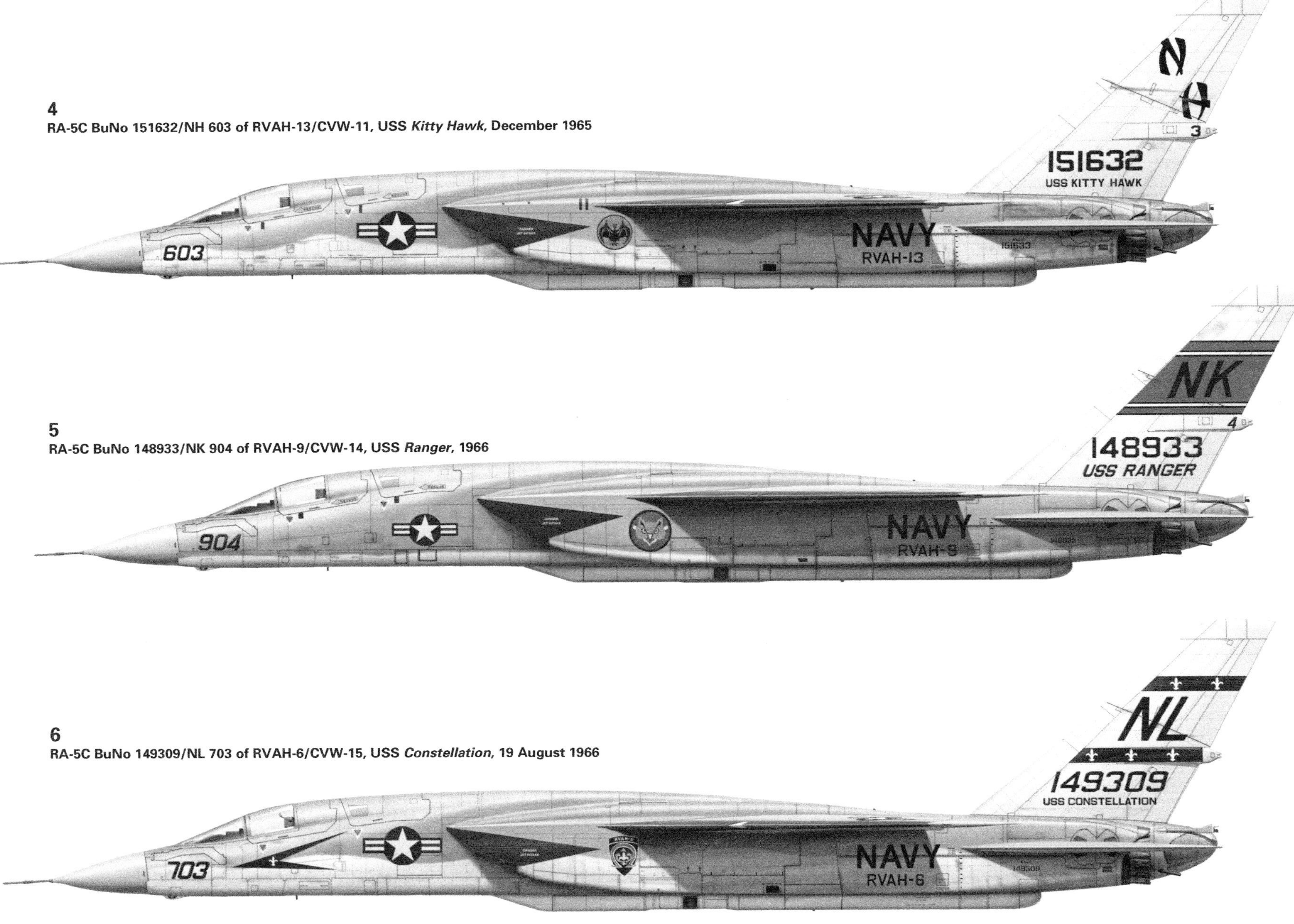

4
RA-5C BuNo 151632/NH 603 of RVAH-13/CVW-11, USS *Kitty Hawk*, December 1965

5
RA-5C BuNo 148933/NK 904 of RVAH-9/CVW-14, USS *Ranger*, 1966

6
RA-5C BuNo 149309/NL 703 of RVAH-6/CVW-15, USS *Constellation*, 19 August 1966

7
RA-5C BuNo 151727/NH 606 of RVAH-13/CVW-11, USS *Kitty Hawk*, late 1966

8
RA-5C BuNo 151634/NK 125 of RVAH-12/CVW-14 USS *Constellation* August 1967

9
RA-5C BuNo 149283/AA 606 of RVAH-11/CVW-17, USS *Forrestal*, 29 July 1967

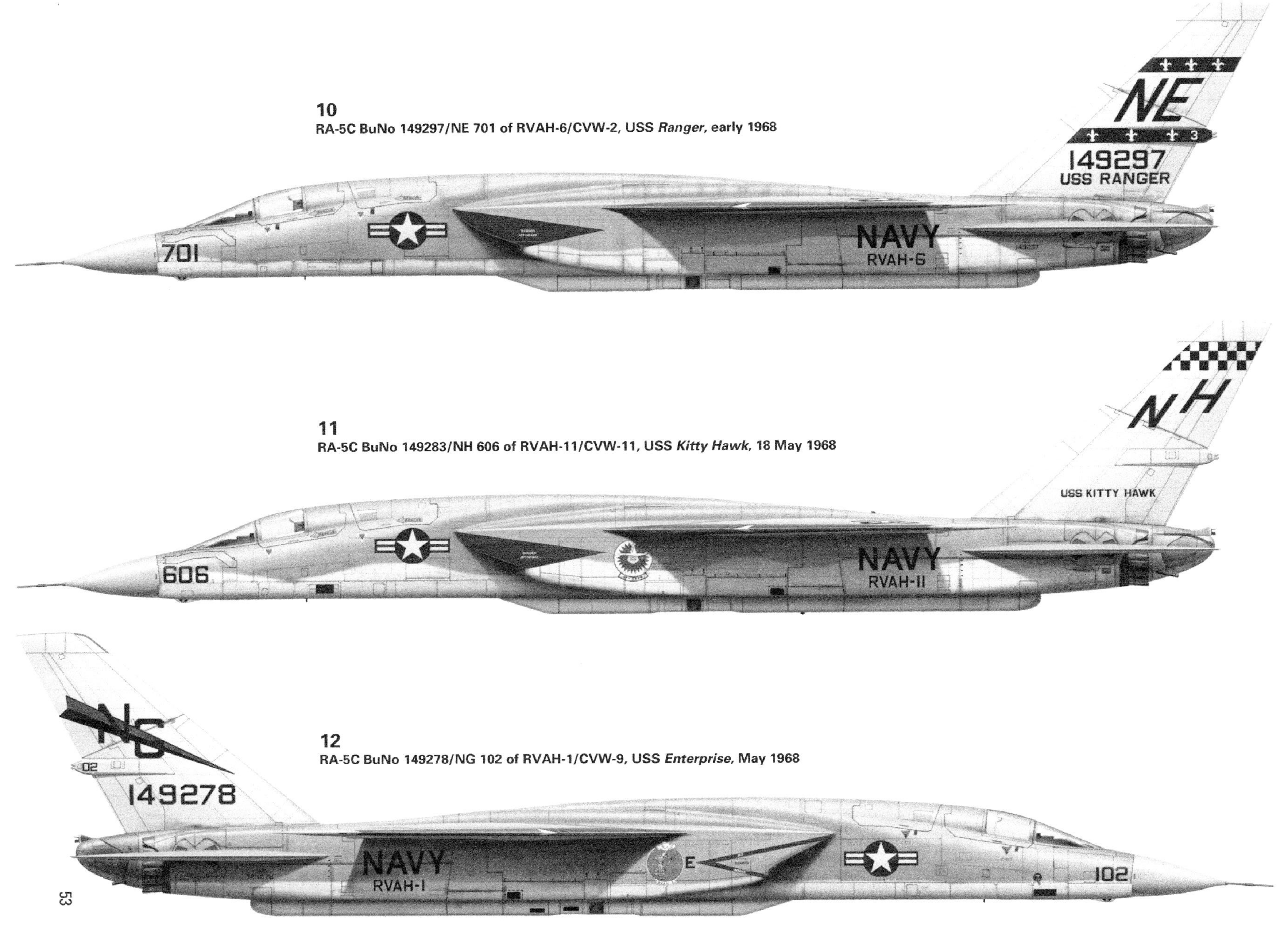

10
RA-5C BuNo 149297/NE 701 of RVAH-6/CVW-2, USS *Ranger*, early 1968

11
RA-5C BuNo 149283/NH 606 of RVAH-11/CVW-11, USS *Kitty Hawk*, 18 May 1968

12
RA-5C BuNo 149278/NG 102 of RVAH-1/CVW-9, USS *Enterprise*, May 1968

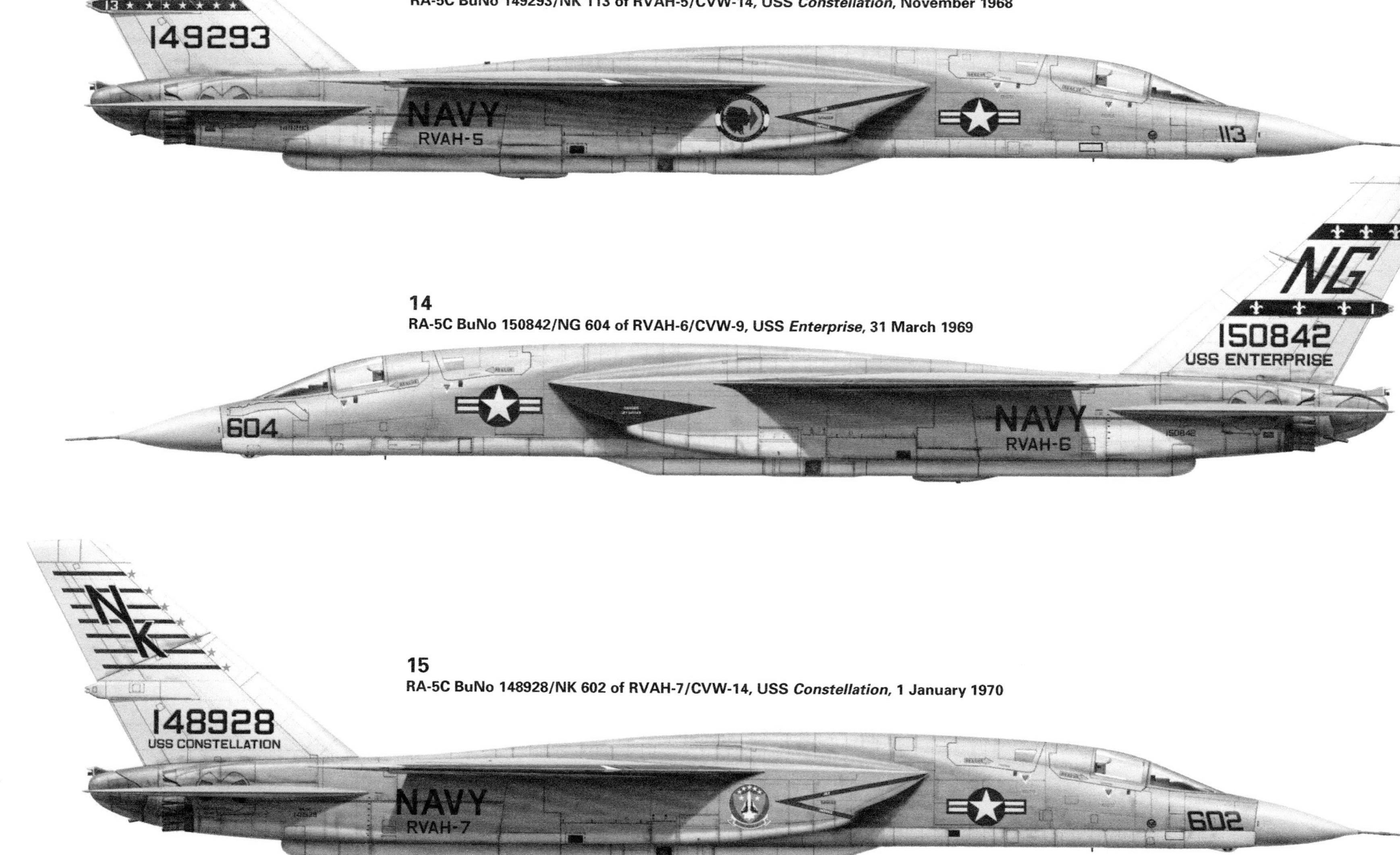

13
RA-5C BuNo 149293/NK 113 of RVAH-5/CVW-14, USS *Constellation*, November 1968

14
RA-5C BuNo 150842/NG 604 of RVAH-6/CVW-9, USS *Enterprise*, 31 March 1969

15
RA-5C BuNo 148928/NK 602 of RVAH-7/CVW-14, USS *Constellation*, 1 January 1970

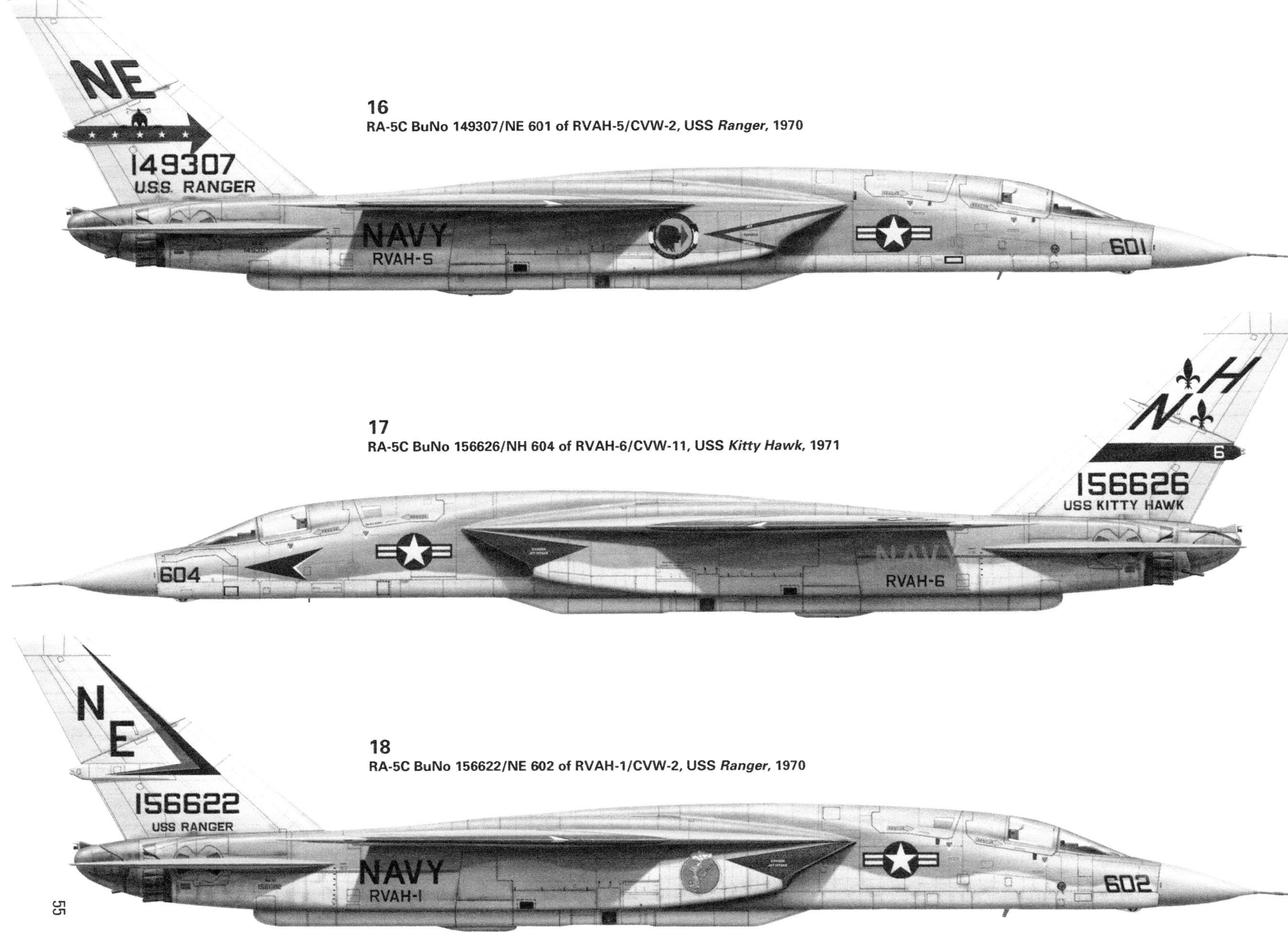

16
RA-5C BuNo 149307/NE 601 of RVAH-5/CVW-2, USS *Ranger*, 1970

17
RA-5C BuNo 156626/NH 604 of RVAH-6/CVW-11, USS *Kitty Hawk*, 1971

18
RA-5C BuNo 156622/NE 602 of RVAH-1/CVW-2, USS *Ranger*, 1970

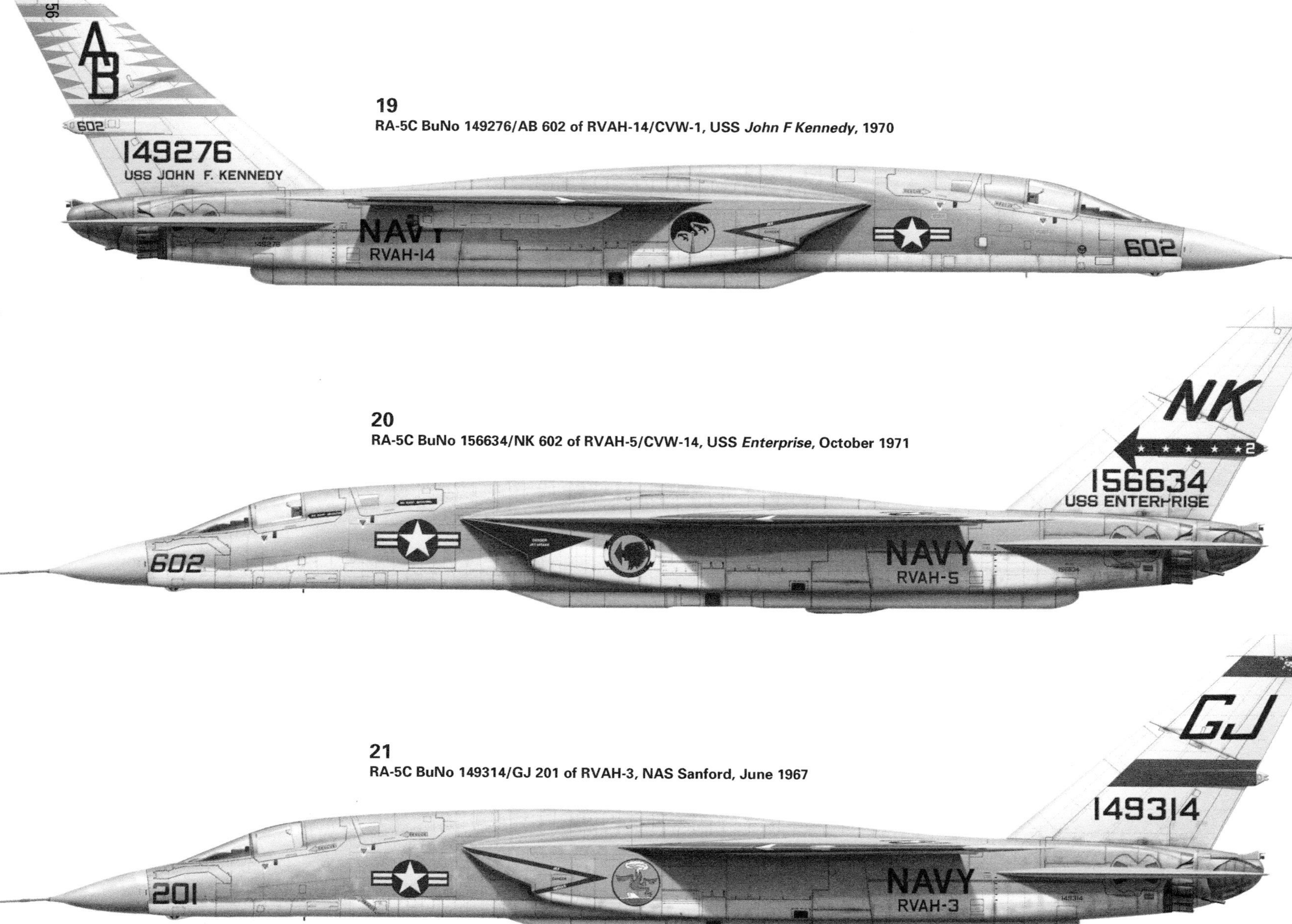

19
RA-5C BuNo 149276/AB 602 of RVAH-14/CVW-1, USS *John F Kennedy*, 1970

20
RA-5C BuNo 156634/NK 602 of RVAH-5/CVW-14, USS *Enterprise*, October 1971

21
RA-5C BuNo 149314/GJ 201 of RVAH-3, NAS Sanford, June 1967

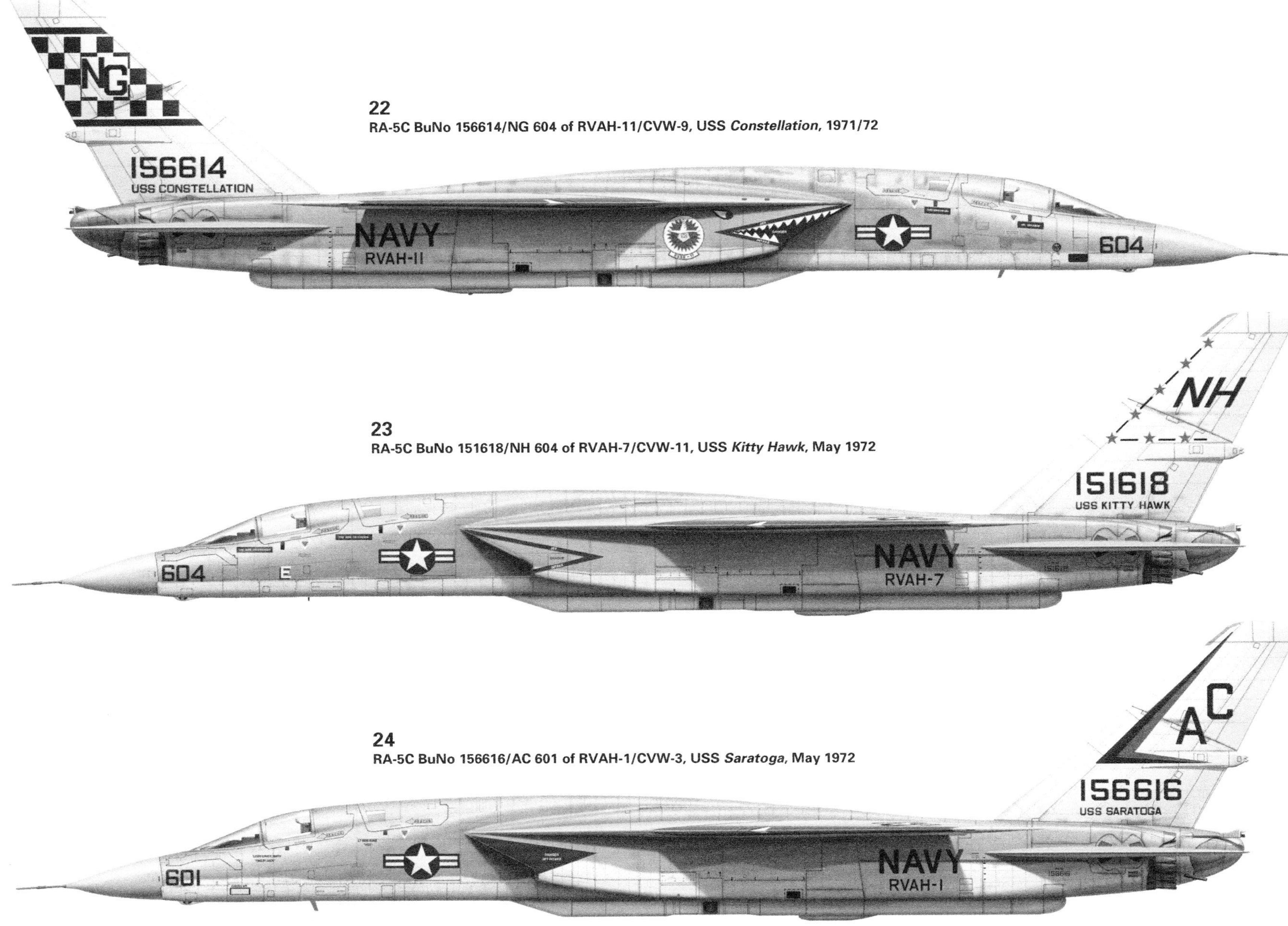

22
RA-5C BuNo 156614/NG 604 of RVAH-11/CVW-9, USS *Constellation*, 1971/72

23
RA-5C BuNo 151618/NH 604 of RVAH-7/CVW-11, USS *Kitty Hawk*, May 1972

24
RA-5C BuNo 156616/AC 601 of RVAH-1/CVW-3, USS *Saratoga*, May 1972

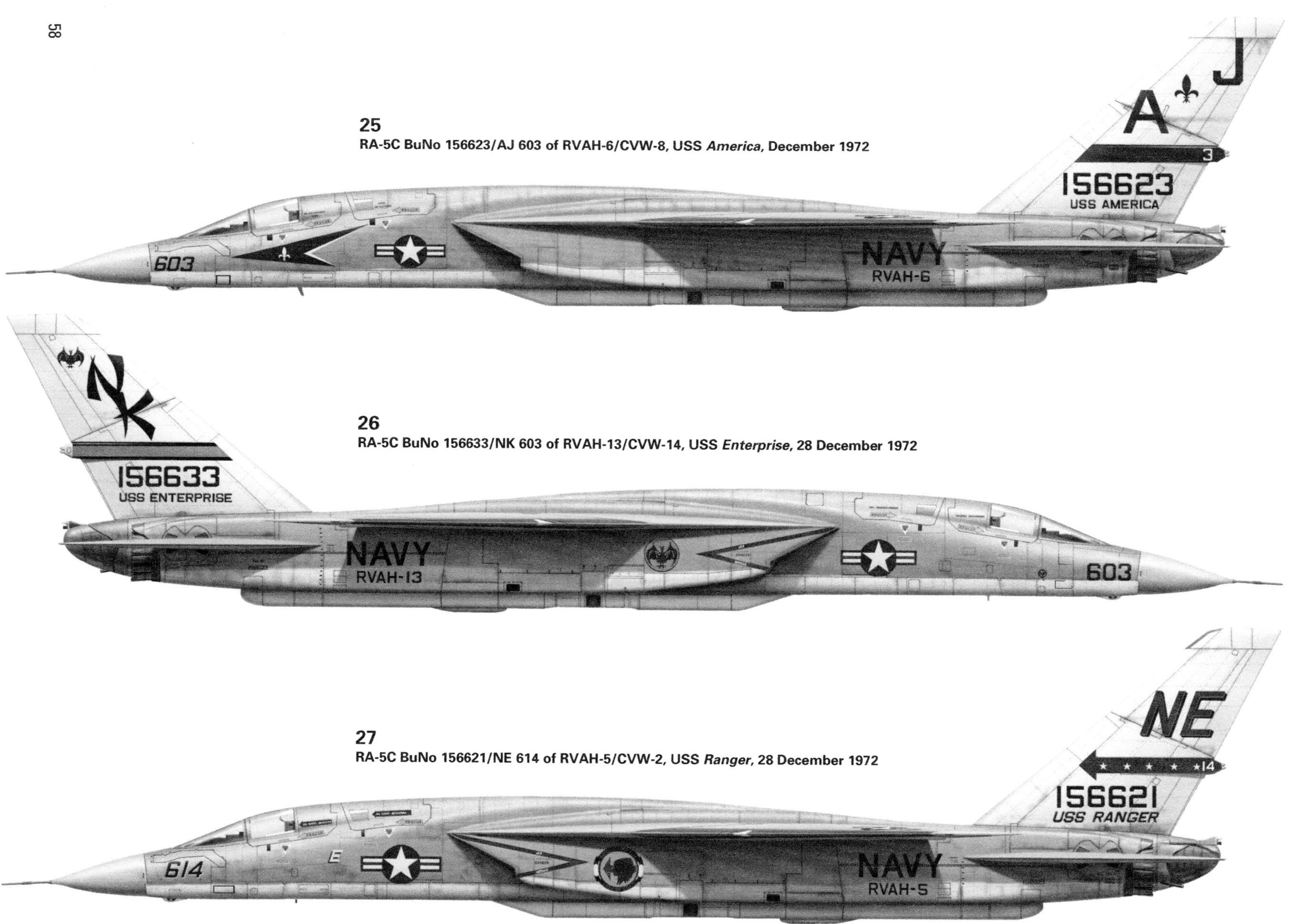

25
RA-5C BuNo 156623/AJ 603 of RVAH-6/CVW-8, USS *America*, December 1972

26
RA-5C BuNo 156633/NK 603 of RVAH-13/CVW-14, USS *Enterprise*, 28 December 1972

27
RA-5C BuNo 156621/NE 614 of RVAH-5/CVW-2, USS *Ranger*, 28 December 1972

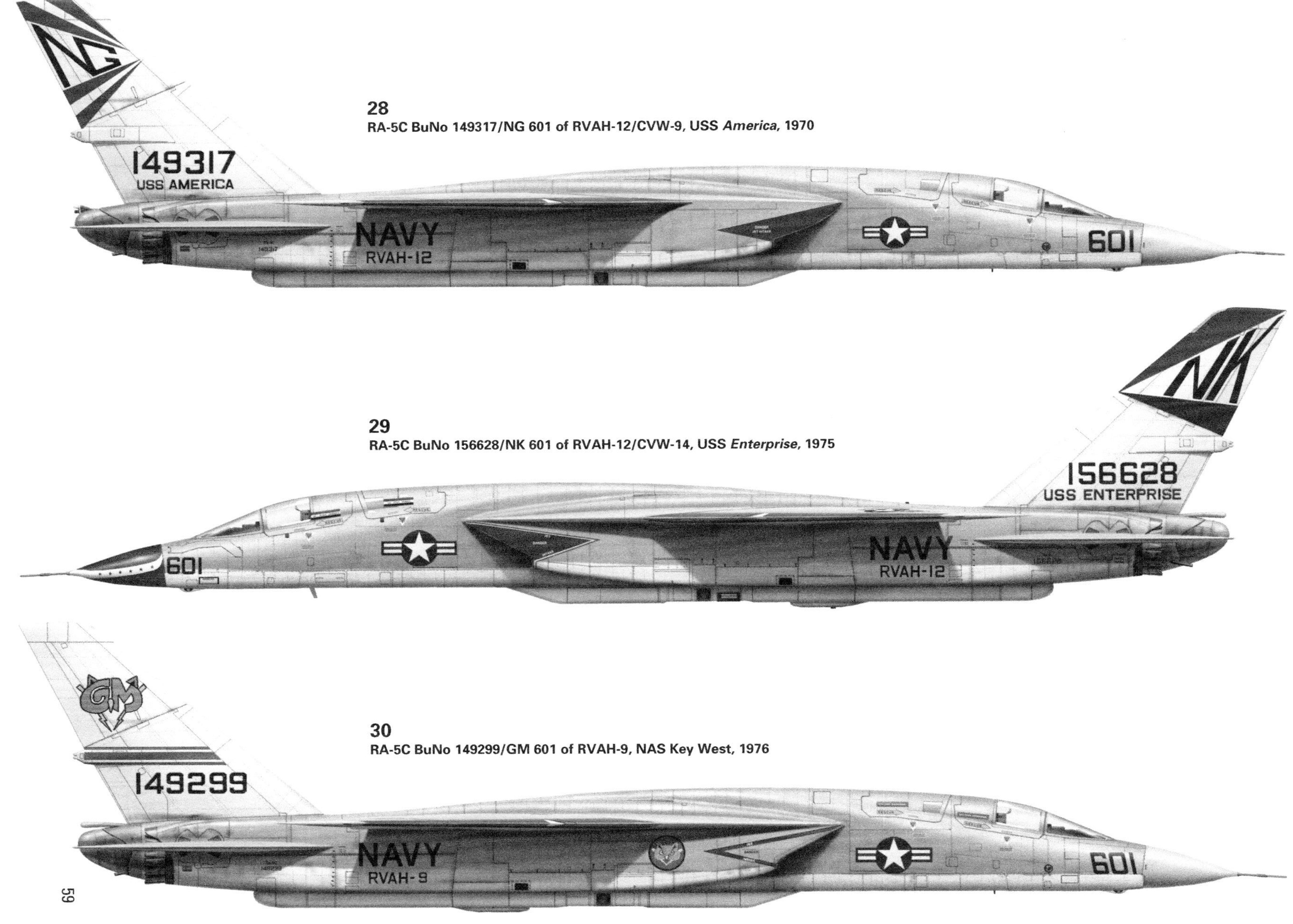

28
RA-5C BuNo 149317/NG 601 of RVAH-12/CVW-9, USS *America*, 1970

29
RA-5C BuNo 156628/NK 601 of RVAH-12/CVW-14, USS *Enterprise*, 1975

30
RA-5C BuNo 149299/GM 601 of RVAH-9, NAS Key West, 1976

1

2

3

4

156623
NH
155716

5

106
105

6

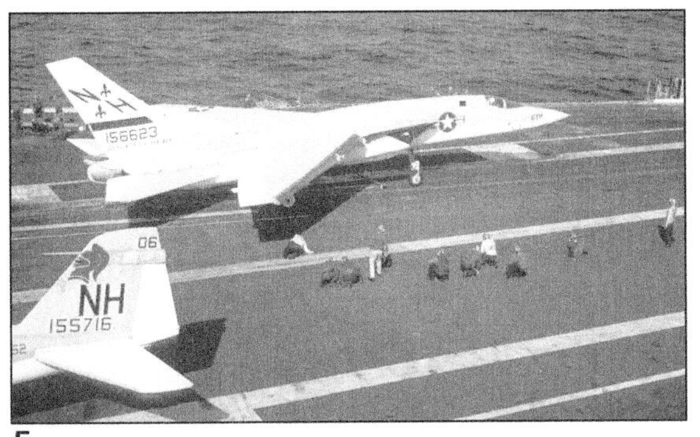

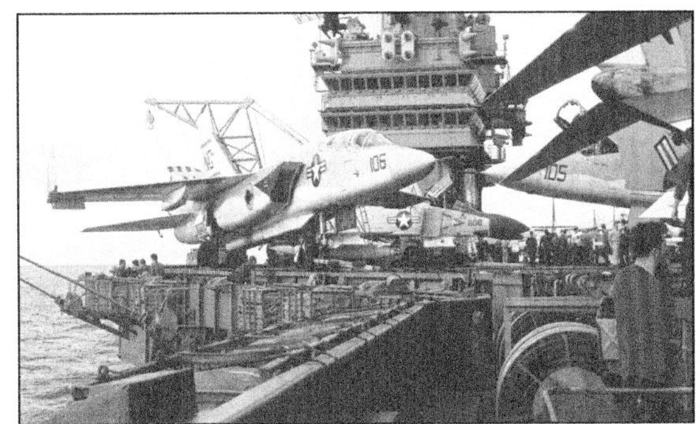

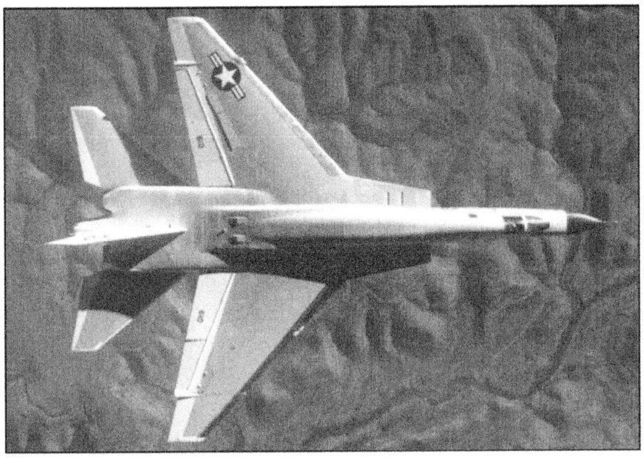

7

AG
156642
601

8

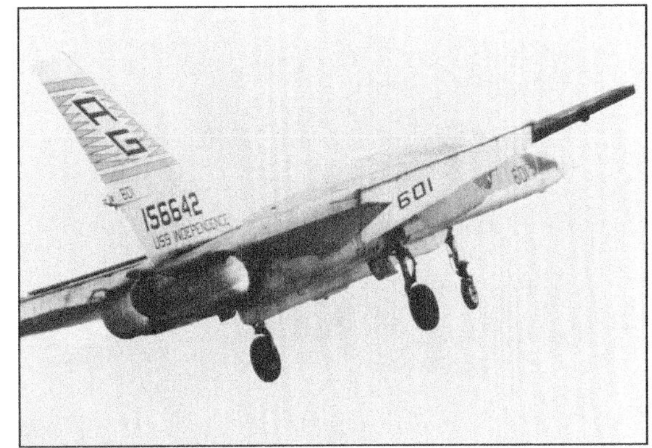

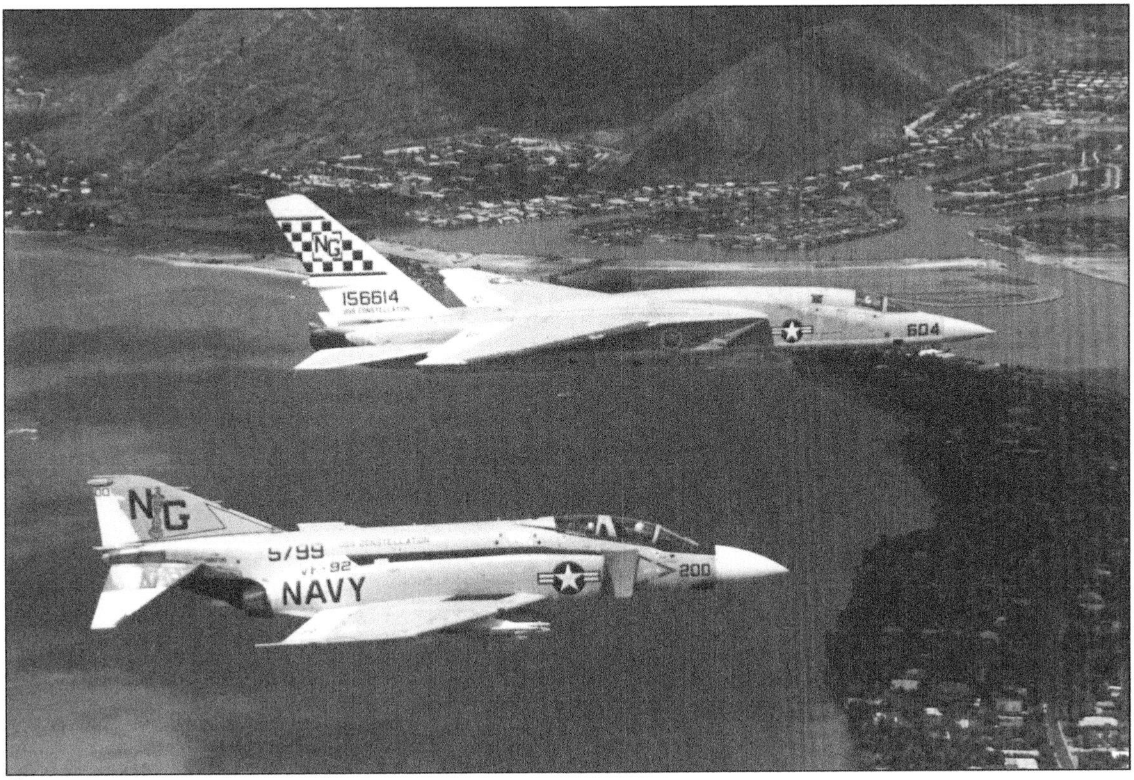
NG
156614
604
NG
5799
VF-92
NAVY
200

9

10

11

12

Capt G W Kimmons (pilot) was commander of Reconnaissance Attack Wing One when he travelled to the NAA factory in Columbus, Ohio, to pick up this new '156 series' Vigilante that was intended for the 1969 London-New York Air Mail Race. Sat behind Kimmons is RAN Lt Cdr Dave Turner, who was one of the initial cadre that had trained at the Columbus factory on the first RA-5Cs. The atomic bomb flash sliding panels that would cover the RAN's windows are clearly visible, as is the pull-out hood for the front canopy. The window panels were used throughout the Vigilante's career to help RANs read the radar scope, but the pilot's hood had little value for reconnaissance, so the rounded plastic pieces and the overhead rail were removed (*Turner*)

was arranged. We'd carry four drop tanks, but would jettison them in the Irish Sea soon after take-off. One of our major problems was how to get into the city while wearing the full-pressure suits we had to wear because of the altitudes we were going to fly at. Then the Navy bureaucracy put a thumbs down on the idea. Very disappointing.'

The unlimited category was won by an RAF Harrier 'jump jet', which had the ability to land at downtown helicopter pads.

The new '156 series' aeroplanes suffered a setback on 27 September 1970. 'Beef' Renner had served as the RAG LSO for several years, and was finally back in a fleet squadron. RVAH-1 was running routine CarQuals off California in preparation for deployment on *Ranger*, Renner flying BuNo 156629 to what at first seemed to be a normal arrested landing. Halfway through the run-out, one of the two attachment points on the A-frame tailhook broke and the 50,000-lb jet lurched to one side. The strain snapped the other attachment point and the Vigilante went off the deck, too fast to stop, too slow to fly. The crew pulled the ejection handles, but they were low, slow and going down fast. Lt Cdr Renner and his RAN, Lt Max Joseph, both died when they hit the sea.

All the Vigilantes, both old and new, were immediately restricted from shipboard operations in the wake of the crash. Extensive investigation soon discovered that the bearing where the hook frame attached to the fuselage did not have any provision for lubrication, resulting in the bearings being stress-fractured. A procedure for lubricating the bearings was developed, and the RA-5C was cleared to go back to sea.

An exceedingly smooth and clean RA-5C (devoid of all markings bar the national insignia), with the canoe not installed and 'race tuned' J79-GE-10 engines fitted. Higher Navy authority decided, unfortunately, not to enter the race, as this Vigilante surely would have been the winner instead of the Royal Air Force Harrier GR 1 which took the prize (*Turner*)

The new Vigilantes taken on deployment by RVAH-1 on *Ranger* and RVAH-6 on *Kitty Hawk* had the shiny factory paint scheme with a wavy demarcation line and lettering in pale blue. They slipped into the routine as 1970 became 1971.

The two largest aeroplanes to routinely operate from aircraft carriers sit alongside each other during *Enterprise's* 1969 combat cruise. The A-3 and the A-5 both had folding tails, as well as the more usual folding wings. Both landed weighing 50,000 lbs, and both started their fleet careers as nuclear bombers, before finding other roles (*EBAL*)

BLACK TRACK

Night PECM missions during the 'Highway Patrol' period were typically quiet sorties – boring enough that the 'Vigi' pilots would let the autopilot fly the jet so that they could in turn help the RAN write down navigational fixes from TACAN stations. All the way north along the border, the ALQ would be quiet, with only an occasional beep from search radars. Then, at the end of the route near the Mu Gia Pass, as the RA-5C started to turn around, the warning gear would come alive with pulsing strobes on the threat display and undulating warbles in the headphones – every indication of tracking AAA and imminent SAM launches. The crew's pulse would shoot up as they prepared to evade missiles or flak. Then it would all suddenly stop just as the wings levelled after 180 degrees of turn. The enemy knew that the information gathered by the PECM was not especially accurate when the aircraft was turning.

One night on the Black Track over Laos, a crew from RVAH-6 had excitement of another kind. Air Force B-52s were effectively, if inefficiently, carpet-bombing North Vietnamese Army and Viet Cong storage and troop areas in South Vietnam, Cambodia and Laos. Each bomber dropped 84 500- and 24 750-lb bombs, and the B-52s flew in cells of three. A total of 324 bombs with a combined weight of 90 tons from just one cell created utter devastation in mile-wide swathes. Captured soldiers reported that B-52 attacks terrified them. These massive bomb drops were called *Arc Light*, and as a precaution before bombs away, announcements were made over the radio on guard channel which all friendly aircraft monitored.

The author was flying blissfully along when guard channel blared, '*Arc Light, Arc Light*, coordinates north 1722, east 10605, *Arc Light, Arc Light*'. He paid little attention, as *Arc Light* warnings came frequently.

Moments later, his backseater, Lt Cdr 'Bull' Davis, announced on the intercom, 'We're there!' Powell looked up over his shoulder, and there were the black silhouettes of six B-52s. He lit the afterburners, rolled, pulled and dived fast to get out of the way. Safely away, they looked back to see explosion after explosion rippling through the jungle – so close together they formed a solid carpet of flame and fire.

A measure of the difficulties and restrictions placed on reconnaissance missions over North Vietnam by politicians in Washington is portrayed in this cruise patch made up by RVAH-6 in 1971 (*Conrad*)

TROLLING AT QUAN LANG

One of the most remarkable photographs ever taken by a Vigilante happened accidentally on 1 March 1971. 'Field Goal 602' was assigned a reconnaissance route that crossed over itself in order to get the tasked coverage of the Song Ca and a smaller river. The entire route was easily inside the SAM envelopes around Vinh. At Vigilante speeds, Lt Cdr Barry Gastrock and Lt Emerson Conrad were back over the river juncture at Hung Nghia, heading south, less than four minutes after crossing the same village westbound. AAA had only been sporadic, and there had been no missile warnings when Conrad saw a flash in his viewfinder and yelled, 'Pull up!' Gastrock yanked hard. They heard a whumpf, and were thrown against the seat-straps.

Framed under the wing of a CVW-2 A-7B Corsair II equipped with an AGM-45 Shrike anti-radiation missile, an RVAH-5 Vigilante is catapulted from the deck of *Ranger* in late 1969. A plane guard SH-3A Sea King from HC-1 Det 1 can just be seen in the distance (*Mersky*)

Speeding toward the coast, they watched and listened for possible damage to their Vigilante. There was none. At 600 knots, it did not take long to reach the waters of the Tonkin Gulf, and the jet soon went feet wet and headed back to *Kitty Hawk* for a routine recovery.

In the IOIC, a photo-interpreter cranked the five inch-wide film from one massive spool to another across the lighted area of the viewing table and stopped. He called others to look. Soon that segment was cut out and positive image prints made. Perfectly framed in the vertical camera was an SA-2 missile still under boost. The crew was called to see the near miss. As best they could figure out, since there was no terrain visible in the frame, the SAM passed under the RA-5C at the last target as Gastrock had banked hard for home. Knowing the focal length of the camera, and the size of a SA-2 warhead, photogrammeters computed that the missile had passed 104 ft from the jet's belly. No one knows why it did not detonate.

The frequent bombing of choke points along the trail created ten-mile wide areas of devastation that were as desolate and crater-pocked as the surface of the moon. The mountain passes of Mu Gia, Nape and Ban Karai had to be seen to be believed. The Air Force, Marines and Navy would attack them all day and into the night, but in the morning, when the Vigilantes brought back fresh photographs, the craters would be filled in, there were multiple dikes and roadways and fresh tyre tracks.

Since the jungle-covered ridges around the passes were called mountains, and they had steep slopes, a jacket patch was made with crossed snow skis, a mountain silhouette and the legend, *Ski Mu Gia, 100 Beautiful Trails*.

In March 1971, 'Protective Reaction' strikes were allowed. Stripped of political niceties, 'Protective Reaction' was justification for attacks in North Vietnam. If a reconnaissance mission was shot at, US forces were allowed to 'react' to 'protect' the unarmed aircraft. The RVAH squadrons called it 'trolling for flak and SAMs, with ourselves as bait'.

Blue Tree missions had shown an airfield under construction at Quan Lang, on the Song Ca River, less than 20 miles from Vinh. Lt Cdr Gastrock and Lt Conrad of RVAH-6 were to plan and lead a *Blue Tree*. The number of supporting aircraft from CVW-11 would have made a

This amazing photograph was taken by the forward-firing oblique camera during a mission over North Vietnam. The forward oblique ran all the time when over land. Its rate of firing was slow, and the pictures taken could later be used to reconstruct the route of flight in the event of an automatic navigation failure. The small black clouds are AAA bursts at 13,000 ft. When exploding that far in front of the RA-5C, the flak was probably barrage fire, which saw gunners attempting to fill the sky with chunks of shrapnel that the Vigilante would then fly into at high speed (*Wattay*)

decent size Alpha strike. Like so many *Blue Tree* missions, conditions had to be exactly right, and they briefed the elaborate mission, only to be cancelled, rescheduled again for another brief and another scrub and another brief and cancel. They had briefed Quan Lang so many times, the basics were video-taped. When someone new was assigned to fly with them, he was told to watch the tape.

At last, on 22 April, after the airfield was complete and a pair of MiGs were parked there, 'Field Goal 602' and the supporting players were actually launched.

PECM and earlier reconnaissance had reported 29 radars, including seven of the deadly fire-control 'Fan Songs', located there. The 'Dynamic Duo' of Gastrock and Conrad had flown over the site a month before, when they unintentionally photographed a SAM in their vertical camera. Fully loaded with ordnance, the A-6s, F-4s and A-7s of CVW-11 were waiting off the coast as the Vigilante made a high speed, low pass down the centre of the new runway, then pulled up and came back in the opposite direction. The bait was too much to resist, and the Vietnamese gunners opened up and the SAM radars went active. The attack aircraft 'reacted' and rolled in to 'protect' the Vigilante. When they left, and the smoke cleared, both MiGs and most of the SAM and AAA sites had been destroyed, along with a jet starter unit, a fire truck and a road grader.

Not all work done by Vigilantes was serious. Carriers would make a cruise book for their deployment, illustrated with pictures of the crew and shipboard activities. During work-ups, the RA-5C would have colour film loaded in oblique cameras set at a shallow angle, and word would go out to all the units that if a 'Vigi' joined on you that day, tighten your formation and smile. The $14 million dollar Kodak took great photos.

With two or three carriers operating in the Tonkin Gulf at any one time, mistakes were made. One clear day, a nugget A-7 pilot from the 'big deck' carrier *Kitty Hawk* landed by mistake on the much smaller 27C class USS *Hancock* (CVA-19). An alert Vigilante crew heard the radio conversation and headed for the carrier with cameras firing. By the time the embarrassed pilot returned to CVA-63, 12 x 16-inch glossy prints of a lone A-7 parked amid the aircraft of *Hancock's* air wing were in all the ready rooms, on the captain's and admiral's bridge and CAG's office.

GETTING IN

Never a problem on board ship or at home base, the special boarding ladders (the black-painted indexes on the cockpit edges at the canopy

The legendary photograph of the SA-2 missile that passed just 104 ft below 'Field Goal 602'. The most likely theory as to why the SAM did not explode is that the missile had not reached its arming time when it shot past the wildly jinking RA-5C (*Conrad*)

This new '156 series' RA-5C was delivered to RVAH-6 in time to participate in the unit's 1970-71 *WestPac* aboard *Kitty Hawk* (*Mersky*)

seam showed where to hang the ladder) the Vigilante (and the A-4 Skyhawk) required were usually not available when the aircraft had to divert into Da Nang or other air bases in Vietnam or Thailand. The procedure for getting into the RA-5C was elaborate, and required physical dexterity. Before shutting down the engines, and losing hydraulic pressure, the pilot had to remember to trim as far nose down as possible. This put the trailing edge of the big horizontal stabiliser at its lowest position.

Then, when the crew came back to the aeroplane, they would open both canopies with switches on the side of the nose, walk back to the tail and, with skill worthy of an acrobat, jump, pull and turn themselves onto the stabiliser. This task was difficult enough without the torso harness, life preserver, survival vest, hard hat, map bag and G-suit getting in the way. Once up, it was easy to stand, take a short step onto the relatively flat fuselage and walk forward to the RAN's canopy, grasping the edge for stability while inching forward on the narrow sill on the cockpit edge. The RAN could then step into his cockpit. The poor pilot had still to grasp the edge of the back cockpit with one hand, reach forward to his own canopy with the other and take a giant stride to get his left foot on his canopy sill, pause spreadeagled nine feet off the ground, and hop-shift his weight forward – not much fun on a windy, rainy night.

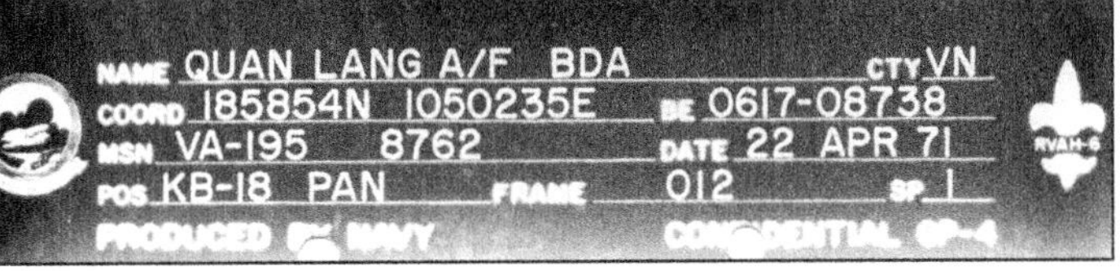

A BDA photograph of the airfield at Quan Lang, taken by Lt Cdr Gastrock and Lt Conrad after the 'protective reaction' *Blue Tree* attacks by CVW-11 aircraft from *Kitty Hawk* on 22 April 1971 (*Conrad*)

Enterprise, with the 'Savage Sons' of RVAH-5 on board, relieved both *Kitty Hawk* and *Ranger*. In October 1971, RVAH-5 Vigilante BuNo 156634 flew into the water while on a training flight, killing the squadron CO, Cdr L R 'Bud' Everett, and RAN, Lt Cdr Paul Stokes. This was the first RA-5C loss in *WestPac* since March 1969

For three months *Enterprise* was the only 'big deck' in the Tonkin Gulf until *Constellation*, with RVAH-11 'Checkertails' embarked, arrived for the transition to an entirely new phase of the air war.

The attacks on the Ho Chi Minh trail destroyed thousands of trucks and tons of supplies, but for every truck destroyed and every ton of supplies burned, two, three or four more would come into Haiphong from Soviet Bloc ships and start down the trail.

The US Navy lost 130 aircraft and their crews during the bombing halt, which lasted from November 1968 to early 1972, and the start of *Linebacker* operations. In the same period, some 100 'Protective Reaction' strikes were flown off aircraft carriers into North Vietnam.

LINEBACKER FINALE

In March 1972, the North Vietnamese army launched a major offensive across the DMZ. The South Vietnamese needed extensive American assistance to hold their ground, and with the Paris peace talks obviously going nowhere, President Nixon ordered a large scale air campaign against the North. Operation *Linebacker* began on 9 May when Navy A-6s and A-7s dropped mines across the entrances to Haiphong Harbour, as well as the harbours of Cam Pha, Hon Gay, Vinh and Thanh Hoa. The mines' activation was delayed so foreign ships could leave.

The Vigilante's role in this operation was overhead imagery to accurately plot the mines' placement. RVAH-7 aboard *Kitty Hawk* and RVAH-1 on *Saratoga* (that carrier's only trip to Vietnam) had arrived on station as scheduled, and they would overlap with RVAH-11 on CVA-64 until the 'Checkertails' departed following eight months in *WestPac*.

America, with RVAH-6 assigned, was within weeks of deploying to the Mediterranean from its homeport of Norfolk, Virginia. When the decision to initiate *Linebacker* was reached, all personnel were recalled and CVW-8 embarked in a hurry. *America* sailed within days, heading for the tip of Africa, the Indian Ocean and its third spell on *Yankee Station*. By the autumn, and with the arrival of *Enterprise* (RVAH-13) and *Ranger* (RVAH-5), five of the US Navy's biggest and best carriers were in position to cut off all supplies coming into North Vietnam from abroad, and destroy military stockpiles and targets already in the country. Every worthwhile target in the North would be attacked. Vigilantes continued to fly missions into high threat areas, conducting dangerous BDA sorties.

Three-and-a-half years of restricted bombing had given the North Vietnamese time to significantly improve their defences. There were more guns, more SAMs and more MiGs (mostly dangerous, supersonic MiG-21s), and no shortage of experienced gunners, missile operators and pilots trained to use them. The stage was set for a fierce battle.

This late-build RA-5C participated in RVAH-5's fifth, and last, combat deployment to Vietnam, which commenced on 16 November 1972. The unit had seen action from *Ranger's* flight deck on three of these cruises. BuNo 156632 was put on display at Sanford airport in May 2003 (*Mersky*)

A '156 series' Vigilante of RVAH-3 rides port bow cat two during Carrier Qualifications (CQ) aboard USS *Coral Sea* (CVA-43). Although the *Midway* class carrier was deemed to be too small to operate RA-5Cs on a permanent basis, the vessel was fine for CQs. The initial qualification was for ten day and six night landings. This was increased for pilots going out to deployed squadrons. There was no actual requirement for RANs to be 'CarQualed', but in keeping with the crew concept, they went along for the ride during the long practice landing sessions ashore, and then stayed with the pilot for traps on the ship. A good RAN could steady a nervous pilot. Experienced RAG instructors 'CarQualed' with nugget pilots (*EBAL*)

Photographed in June 1971, RA-5C BuNo 156613 wears the GJ tail code of the 'recce RAG' (*Mersky*)

From the beginning of the Vigilante programme, all pilots sent to RVAH units already had fleet experience in other aeroplane types prior to flying the RA-5C. RANs, however, were a more normal mix of experienced aircrewmen and graduates fresh out of Training Command. In 1969 this changed, with the first newly-winged pilots arriving in the Vigilante training squadron, RVAH-3. These 'Nuggets' were not only a select group, they also received extra training before reporting to the fleet.

Despite initial qualms, the nugget programme proved very successful. Graduates included Jim Flaherty, who later led F-14-equipped VF-211 and became commander of all Atlantic Fleet Fighter Squadrons, Rob Weber (a second generation 'Hooter', his father having flown AJ Savages in VC-9), who commanded A-6 squadron VA-35 and was later captain of the aircraft carrier USS *John F Kennedy* (CV-67), and Joe Dyer, who

RVAH-3 BuNo 156630 powers away from the flight deck, each J79 in full afterburner putting out 18,000 lbs of thrust. This aeroplane was later transferred to RVAH-1, and it was lost when the crew ejected near NAS Albany on 1 March 1972. One Vigilante pilot's description of a catapult shot was as follows;

'The catapult fires. The weight of your chest forces out a grunt. You strain your neck trying to pull your head off the rest – if you succeed you will have to eject, as something has gone wrong. Some 70,000 lbs of aeroplane is accelerating to 170 mph. As the "Vigi" clears the deck, 3000 lbs of hydraulic pressure in the nose gear extends the oleo strut hard enough to vibrate the nose and make the instrument panel blur – barely noticed in the day, but providing moments of confused terror at night. You can now lean forward, reach with your left hand and raise the landing gear lever, pulling the throttles back from afterburner to military power' (*EBAL*) became a three-star admiral after directing the Navy Test Center at Patuxent River.

For some of the 'Vigi' nuggets their first missions would be over North Vietnam during *Linebacker*. One such individual was Lt(jg) Paul Habel (a quasi-nugget, he had spent a year instructing in the same training unit that he had graduated from), who recalled his first mission with RVAH-11;

RVAH-11 Vigilantes perform some close formation work with F-4Js from VF-92. Flying off *Constellation* on 10 May 1972, VF-92 and VF-96 shot down seven MiGs between them. The lead RA-5C in this shot, BuNo 156609, lost its fuel cans during a cat shot from CVA-64 on 21 May 1973 and the RVAH-12 crew had to eject after losing control of the jet. The second Vigilante in the formation, BuNo 156610, was stricken in Rota, Spain, on 31 October 1978 presumably after a heavy landing. It was deployed with RVAH-12 aboard *Saratoga* at the time, the unit conducting the Vigilante's very last Mediterranean cruise (*EBAL*)

'It was to Mu Gia Pass, way up the back side of North Vietnam – one of the upper starts of the Ho Chi Minh Trail. So down we go from 15,000 ft! I'm thinking "Into the valley of darkness rode the 600". But it was blue skies and really pretty scenery – looked like the Smokey Mountains. All I knew was that I wanted to go as fast as that "Vigi" would carry me. I put my left foot up on the throttles to push them beyond max burner – put a permanent bend in the throttle levers. Well, not literally, but that's what I was thinking.

'Now remember our "Heavy Three" training – "you have to get a visual recce for the debrief" – even though we had 400 cameras running, pointing in every direction. So I noted the valley floor – it had ten million pock-marks. Light brown bomb craters – everything else was lush jungle green. This was the Ho Chi Minh Trail, and US forces had dropped 200 billion Mk 80 series bombs on it. I'd have bet the iron content there was greater than in the Masabi Range in Minnesota. There was no flak – or I didn't see any – or the gunners weren't calibrated for the Vigi's speed, or so I had been briefed – this was my first combat hop – and our "defensive" eyes, the fighter escort, didn't call any. By combat standards it was, after the fact, a milk run.'

RVAH-13's Lt(jg) Russ Campbell went to Vinh on his first combat flight. He had the volume on his ALQ warning system set so high, and so many fire-control radars emitted, that he did not hear any radio calls while over the beach. Back on *Enterprise*, when he learned this, Campbell worried that he may have missed some verbal warnings. Ernie Christensen, a former *Blue Angels* demonstration pilot who had been his escort in a Phantom II, said, 'Don't worry, kid, they couldn't have hit you, you were all over the sky'.

During his first trip near heavily defended Haiphong, RVAH-6's Lt(jg) Wes Rutledge had the escorting F-4 pilot call, '"Field Goal" flight, cease burner so I can keep up'. Rutledge rapidly replied, 'No-no, not now'.

On 7 May 1972, two days before *Linebacker* officially began, Cdr Ron Polfer and Lt(jg) Joe Kernan were in the first Vigilante to be lost due to enemy action since March 1969. Cdr Polfer had completed two tours and 200 missions as a Phantom II pilot, before becoming the XO of RVAH-7 on *Kitty Hawk*. Their mission was BDA on a truck park alongside the Dragon's Jaw Bridge near Thanh Hoa. Flying at 600 knots and 4500 ft, they were hit by heavy AAA and ejected from their flaming RA-5C (BuNo 151618). Both men were captured and released with the last group of PoWs eight months later. Cdr Polfer resumed his career as the CO of RVAH-6, and Joe Kernan later became Mayor of South Bend Indiana, and then the Lieutenant Governor of Indiana.

June 1972 saw a massive pullout of US troops from South Vietnam. In the North, the air war continued hot and heavy.

A view of the notorious Thanh Hoa bridge being bombed. During their debriefs, attack pilots would normally say that the target was obscured in smoke and dust. And the smoke and dust was the reason why Vigilante pilots had to wait ten to fifteen minutes before going in to carry out post-strike photography (*Wattay*)

Flying with the 'Smoking Tigers' of RVAH-1 from *Saratoga*, the tactical crew of LCDR Chuck Smith and Lt(jg) Larry Kunz became the penultimate Vigilante to be lost in South-east Asia. On an earlier mission over North Vietnam, Smith had looked down at his INS readouts only to see the steering bar pegged to the side and distance at over 200 miles, instead of the next target. '"Kooner"', he asked on the intercom, 'where am I?' Kunz' reply became a classic. 'Well, you're eight feet in front of me, going faster than hell . . . and I'm working on the rest'.

The sailors in the maintenance department added the nicknames they had for this colourful pilot/RAN combination below their normal names on the side of BuNo 156616. Smith became 'Smilin' Jack', after the old comic book hero pilot, and Kunz, 'BDT'. He claimed it was taken from the squadron's insignia, and stood for 'Big Deadly Tiger', but in reality it stood for 'Big Dumb Texan'.

Their next adventure was not a happy one. On 7 June, during a reconnaissance of the anchorages in the islands where foreign merchant ships moored to offload their cargo into lighters for transfer into Haiphong, their RA-5C was skewered by a SAM. Coming in at 200 ft and high speed over the Tonkin Gulf, Smith had just popped up to 3000 ft for the photo run when the ALQ gear warned of a missile launch. Evasive manoeuvres left and right were to no avail, and the SA-2 went into and through the fuselage. The missile did not explode or, as Smith states, 'I would not be here telling the story.'

The starboard engine lost power immediately. Smith turned for deep water, and as he lit the afterburner on the other engine it also flamed out. Electrical power went and the flight controls froze. The crew ejected a half-mile southeast of the city and landed 200 hundred yards apart in the water between the islands. Their F-4 escort (flown by a USAF pilot on exchange duty) reported them down, and the A-7E Corsair II ResCAP from VA-37 'Bulls' began bombing and strafing the shore gunners. Two SH-3 Sea

Lt Cdr Chuck Smith had both his name and his nickname – 'Smilin' Jack', after the old comic book hero – applied beneath the forward cockpit of BuNo 156616. He and his RAN, Lt(jg) Larry Kunz, nicknamed 'BDT' were serving with RVAH-1 on *Saratoga* at the time. On 7 June 1972, their 'Vigi' was literally skewered by a SAM and they were forced to eject over Haiphong Harbour (*Smith*)

RVAH-11's RA-5C BuNo 156605 departs *Constellation's* bow cat one on 25 April 1972. The unit, along with the rest of CVW-9, was participating in Operation *Freedom Train* at the time, which was in turn replaced by *Linebacker I* on 9 May (*Mersky*)

Kings of HC-7 (call-signs 'Big Mother 66' and '67') arrived and snatched Smith from the water. The SH-3's mini-gun was firing inches from his face as he hung in the hoist.

A para-rescue swimmer leaped to assist Kunz, but he jumped from too great a height and collapsed a lung on impact with the water. Kunz swam over and helped his 'rescuer' into the sling, before he too was hoisted aboard. The gunfire from both sides did not stop until the SH-3s left the area 50 minutes after the ejections.

The following day when Kunz learned another RAN in the squadron had turned in his wings, he angrily said to Smith, 'Hey, wasn't it you and me that got shot down?'

By October the air war against the North was won. Munitions were not getting into the country, MiGs had been downed in record numbers (eight on 10 May alone), and the survivors were doing little flying because of a lack of fuel. Pilots going over Haiphong and Hanoi reported virtually no opposition – the enemy was out of ammunition and out of SAMs.

But then the politicians and diplomats took over. In one of those moves fighting men cannot understand, President Nixon ordered a bombing halt to show the North Vietnamese negotiators in Paris 'good faith'. As with previous halts, the North Vietnamese pretended to honour the settlement, while all the while restocking and rearming.

The intransigence of the leaders in Hanoi forced the US to resume the bombing – and resume it with a vengeance. B-52s attacked military targets throughout the country, including some inside the Hanoi and Haiphong city limits. The 11 days of the 'Christmas Campaign' were the fiercest period of air fighting in history. Fifteen of the giant, eight-engined bombers were downed by SAMs, but by the new year any worthwhile target had been destroyed.

The weather two days before Christmas was poor, and a strike group from *America* diverted to the south while the RVAH-6 Vigilante and its escorting F-4J from VMFA-333 went north along the coastal islands on its secondary mission. RA-5C BuNo 156623, call-sign 'Fieldgoal 603', was flown by unit CO, Cdr Jim Thompson, with RAN Lt Emy Conrad.

VMFA-333 'Triple Trey' was the only Phantom II-equipped US Marine Corps squadron to deploy to Vietnam aboard a carrier, and 'Fieldgoal 603's' escort was 'Shamrock 210' flown by unit CO Lt Col John K Cochran and his RIO Maj H S Carr.

Heading east at 2900 ft and 480 knots near the island of Danh Do La, Cdr Thompson saw the Phantom II take a direct hit from an 85 mm AAA shell. The F-4 pitched straight down as the crew ejected, and at that speed and altitude, both men were in the water in seconds. Cochran and Carr were alive, although badly battered by the ejection.

The gunners on shore immediately opened fire on the survivors, so the Vigilante began making low passes in an effort to draw the gunners' attention away from the men in the water. As Conrad described it;

'On some passes I could see the face of the gunner on the quad 23 mm as he was trying to track us. We were so close and moving so fast that the gun was about 45 degrees behind his eyes. Contact was attempted on guard channel with the downed crew. No voice was heard, but we did hear an emergency beeper. I kept telling them to swim south, and that help was coming. The flak, large and small was heavy. I could also see small arms firing along the beach.'

Hearing all the chatter on guard, a Corsair II from VA-86 aboard *Saratoga* arrived. Although the jet was rigged as a tanker, and the pilot had only his cannon, he made strafing runs on the beach where the small arms fire was coming from. Another A-7 with a load of Rockeye bombs was vectored in, and the pilot checked in with 'Fieldgoal 603', who was the on-scene SAR commander. As the A-7 silenced the heaviest gun with its devastating cluster bombs, rescue helicopter 'Big Mother 63' checked in. Its pilot said, 'I've no comms with the survivors, and I'm not permitted to go in without talking to them'.

The Commanding Officer of RVAH-6, Cdr Jim Thompson (left, with the handlebar moustache) and Lt Emy Conrad (complete with a full beard) pose in front of a 'Fleur' Vigilante on *America* in 1972. Behind the Vigilante is a VMFA-333 F-4J. This crew would be instrumental in saving a 'Trip Trey' crew that had been their escort. The hotter the war, the laxer the enforcement of regulations – Conrad only wore the skunk-skin hat to and from the aeroplane, and the rule-busting (for flight crews) beard was barely tolerated. The flight gear of the period included G-suits (Conrad had extra bullets sewn onto his) and the LPA flotation device which has lobes about the waist and neck. Earlier experiences with downed airmen resulted in two multi-channel emergency radios being kept in the survival vest pockets, a snap D-ring for hoisting and a flashing strobe-light worn on the shoulder (*Conrad*)

Cdr Thompson had barely escaped capture after his ejection in 1966, and he knew how desperate Cochran and Carr would be. 'You get in and pick them up right now or I'll drag my tailhook through your rotor blades and see if you have comms when you're in the water with them'.

The 'Big Mother' SH-3 went in and picked up both survivors, although it got five bullet holes in it for its trouble, including one through the main rotor from the still active 37 mm gun on the west peninsula. The two Marines were taken to *America's* sickbay, and the Vigilante crew went down to see them. As Conrad later said;

'It was a wild debrief, as the "Trip Trey" guys were doped up and there was liberal use of medicinal brandy all around. The bad part was my wife heard most of the details within 24 hours, and was very upset because I had been writing home telling her nothing much was happening!'

On 28 December 1972, *Enterprise* was on the Noon to Midnight schedule. The RVAH-13 tactical crew of Lt Cdr Al Agnew, pilot, and Lt Mike Haifley, RAN, had flown on the first launch of the day, and hours later they launched on a second mission in RA-5C BuNo156633.

Al Agnew had come into Vigilantes having previously flown propeller-driven S-2 ASW aircraft, and he had completed a Mediterranean cruise

This photograph of the crash site of 'Shamrock 210' was taken by the forward oblique camera fitted in 'Fieldgoal 603' while the pilot was acting as the on-scene SAR coordinator. Smoke from a large calibre gun is visible on the small peninsula. The two Marine aviators who ejected were picked up by a Navy helicopter (*Conrad*)

with Haifley in RVAH-13. After a turn-around period at NAS Albany, the 'Bats' deployed with CVAN-65 on their fourth combat cruise.

The RHAW gear was eerily silent as they accelerated away from the strike group and went feet dry. Together with their F-4J escort from VF-143, they were headed for a pre-strike reconnaissance of a target near Hanoi. As they flew over the roads and railway lines leading into the city, MiG calls from the *Big Look* airborne early warning aircraft came fast and furious. 'Bandits, bandits. Red, blue, Bullseye and all quadrants. Bandits'.

'Flint River 603' finished its photo run and headed for the Tonkin Gulf in burner. The pilot of the F-4 escort radioed in a conversational tone, '"Flint Zero Three", you better turn right'. As Agnew tells it;

'I was already keyed-up. MiG calls were blaring and aggressive fighter guys were heading our way. I broke hard into a 90-degree turn at 700 knots. There was a loud explosion and the Vigi tumbled. I didn't know there were that many negative Gs in the whole world. I was pressed against the straps and my helmet was against the canopy. I somehow managed to reach one of the alternate ejection handles on the side of my seat. Time warped – first, the canopy seemed to take forever to come off, and the next thing I knew, I was hanging in the parachute. I was surprised that the canopy was white and bright orange.'

Another F-4 crew had seen two smoke trails from 'Atoll' missiles fired by a MiG-21, and watched the RA-5C crash. There was only one ejection. Mike Haifley was killed in either the jet's explosion or the crash.

'It was windless day, so I didn't drift in the chute. A group of peasants working in a rice paddy had to move aside to let me land. They stripped me down to my Hang Ten T-shirt and red undershorts I'd gotten for Christmas a few days previous. They swiped my brand new Seiko watch and then this Vietnamese pulls out a big machete. That scared me worse than anything. But all he did with it was cut my flight boots off.'

Agnew spent time in both the Hanoi Hilton and the camp called the 'Zoo'. In the latter he met Gerry Coffee who, in February 1966, had became the first RVAH-13 pilot to be captured. Al Agnew was released on 29 March 1973. Ironically, he was home before his squadron returned from deployment. 'All things considered, it wasn't worth it'.

'Flint 603' was the only Vigilante downed by a MiG, and the last RA-5C to be lost during the war. This was the 90th (according to official US sources), and last, American aircraft shot down by a MiG during the war. This was also the last of 26 Vigilantes to be lost in South-east Asia.

The effectiveness of *Linebacker II* must be judged against the fact that peace negotiations resumed in Paris on 8 January 1973 which led to the signing of a cease-fire agreement 19 days later, and the release of US PoWs in the weeks that followed.

OTHER PLACES, OTHER MISSIONS

The carrier task forces of the US Navy are the most flexible and adaptable response to crises anywhere in the world. Attack and fighter aircraft may be the power behind the threat, but until the shooting starts, all they can do is train and standby. Reconnaissance is always the first mission launched. What the sensors bring back determine what the next action will be. It is worth noting that the first loss of a US Navy aeroplane in Vietnam was a photo-Crusader doing reconnaissance.

Some of the missions flown by the Vigilante outside the South-east Asia theatre of operations are the subject of this chapter. These are reconnaissance missions that may now be talked about – there are many more which may never be declassified. While not 'combat' in the strictest sense, they were hazardous, with the possibility of opposition very real.

1962 – To Cuba . . . Almost

The RA-5C's first opportunity to go into harm's way came before the aircraft had even been accepted by the Navy. On 13 October 1962, high flying USAF U-2 aeroplanes photographed ballistic missile sites under construction in Cuba. Although the event was kept quiet, two weeks later one of the high-flying aircraft was shot down.

Late that same day, John Fosness, then Vigilante Programme Manager at NAA received a call from the Pentagon at his home. The question asked was, 'Could the two prototype RA-5C's have the test instrumentation removed and be reconfigured with advanced electronic countermeasures, along with the basic cameras?' He replied, yes, and was stunned when his high-ranking caller told him they would have to deploy in 24 hours.

Fosness immediately began calling his people. However, it was a Saturday evening, and many of the engineers and technicians were not at home, but scattered around Columbus, Ohio. He remembers talking to many babysitters, and luckily reaching two groups at parties. By midnight, over 100 had been assembled and given their formidable task.

The aeroplanes were ready on time. The pair of Vigilantes may not have looked the best – 'cosmetics' like paint, had a low priority – but they were operational, with cameras and SLR ready to extend the surveillance of Cuba and the surrounding seas. Plus they had the correct ECM equipment to defeat the newest Soviet radars.

Although held in readiness for two weeks, the prototype RA-5Cs were not used. As the crisis eased, Fosness convinced the Navy that such things as accurate fuel consumption figures for the new model would be good to have, and the two Vigilantes had their instrumentation re-installed and resumed development tests.

This rush job would not be the Vigilante's last involvement with Cuba.

Jiffy Soda

To this day, the US Navy has been reluctant to discuss the missions flown around the perimeter of Cuba. Vigilante crewmembers remember performing flights called *Jiffy Soda*, but are unsure of when they began or when the last one took place. These missions were classified, and not openly talked about. The entry in the flight log book was 'routine training', and there are no open records. It was 'combat' of a different sort. They launched from home base and were back in time for dinner with the family. From NAS Sanford and NAS Albany, the Vigilante would stop in NAS Key West for fuel if needed. Once they were moved to the latter station, Cuba was visible soon after take-off. The missions were short enough that an extra fuelling was no longer required.

A *Jiffy Soda* flight would see the jet fly right around Cuba, with its PECM gathering radar signatures and locations and SLR recording a current image of the coastline and several miles inland, while a 36-inch focal length camera mounted in the oblique station – or sometimes the 18-inch panoramic camera – took high resolution photos to correlate with the IR and SLR. Theoretically, the RA-5C remained in international waters, but several missions were intercepted and trailed by MiGs, and lock-ups by Soviet made fire-control radars were not uncommon.

1967 – *Liberty* Attack

During the Arab-Israeli Six Day War in June 1967, US carriers deployed to the Mediterranean – including one en route to Vietnam – stood by on alert awaiting developments. In June, at a time when the US government was trying to keep a neutral position between Israel and Egypt, USS *Liberty* (AGTR-5), a state-of-the art intelligence gathering ship, was in international waters off the Gaza Strip. Word came to *America* that *Liberty* had been attacked by unidentified jets and ships.

Lt Cdr Ron Pollard was a pilot in RVAH-5;

'*America* launched an armed armada to go out to *Liberty*. I flew the Vigilante with the group. I can still picture the setting. The sea was a complete glassy calm. *Liberty* was listing slightly, with many holes in all parts of the ship. Faint smoke was drifting out of it. After circling for a while, we were ordered back to the ship. Some 34 sailors were killed and 171 injured. The survivors were under orders to never tell the facts of the attack. My film was unloaded and never seen by anyone on the ship.

'None of us could believe it when Israel declared it was a mistake. The facts released in the last few years tell of a deliberate and brutal air attack, and how (US President) Johnson covered it up for political reasons.'

1968 – Capture of the *Pueblo*

Less than one year later, another intelligence ship brought the carriers into action. In January 1968, USS *Pueblo* (AGER-2) was fired upon, boarded and captured by the North Korean Navy. *Ranger* and RVAH-6 had completed their second line period on *Yankee Station* when they were ordered to head north. *Enterprise*, with RVAH-1 on board, was in Sasebo, Japan, at the beginning of their deployment.

Lt Cdr Larry DeBoxtel was the junior pilot in RVAH-6, and had been sent to Cubi to pick up an aeroplane and fly it back to *Yankee Station*. While he and his RAN were in Cubi, *Ranger* sailed for Korea, and they were told to go to NAS Atsugi, in Japan. When they stopped in Kadena, Okinawa, it was already cold. Since their anti-exposure suits were on the ship, they drew flight jackets and thermal underwear from the USAF supply depot (DeBoxtel wore the Air Force style flight jacket with the orange liner for years afterwards).

The legendary SR-71 was then operating from Kadena AFB. The visiting Vigilante drew its usual oohs and aahs. One Air Force officer asked DeBoxtel what the aeroplane did. 'Box' looked around to see who was near and whispered, 'It's the replacement for that', pointing toward the SR-71. The legend of the Vigilante grew.

Both RVAH squadrons flew extensively off the North Korean coast while the rest of the air wing remained clear, standing by in support. The 'Fleurs' tried out their new IR scanners over South Korea during night flights. After a month the situation had quieted down, although *Pueblo* and its crew remained in the hands of the North Koreans. *Enterprise* and *Ranger* headed for the Tonkin Gulf

1969 – EC-121 Down

The North Koreans shot down an EC-121 surveillance aircraft on 15 April 1969, and in a repeat of its 1968 experience, RVAH-6 was again pulled off the line to go to Korea. At least this time it was not in the dead of winter. RVAH-9, aboard *Ranger* (the aircraft carrier the 'Fleurs' had been on the previous time off Korea) joined them. The 'Hooters' had been successfully operating off Vietnam since the end of November.

Flight operations were also a repeat of the *Pueblo* incident. The Vigilantes flew surveillance runs off the coast and the air wing remained ready to go into combat, but the diplomats held sway. When the crisis was considered over, RVAH-9 was at the end of its time in *WestPac* and headed home. After the *Enterprise* fire and the diversion to Korea, RVAH-6 had only two short line periods before it was time to head home too. The squadron was reduced in size back at NAS Albany, and it worked in support of RVAH-3 until getting the first five of the new '156 series' Vigilantes and beginning work-ups to go to sea again.

1971 – Mt Soufriere

The threat for RVAH-6 Vigilantes in late 1971 was not from weapons of war, but Nature herself. Just before Christmas, the squadron duty officer (SDO) was amazed to get a call from CRAW-1 over normal telephone lines asking how many 'up' IR sets (AAS-21 was still classified) the unit had for 'a mission down south'. When the SDO reminded the staffer they were talking on an unsecured line, he laughed and said 'Oh, nothing like that (Cuba). There's a volcano about to erupt in the Caribbean.'

The next morning a 'Fleur' Vigilante took off for NAS Roosevelt Roads, in Puerto Rico, hot refuelled, and flew the first special mission over Mt Soufriere, on St Vincent Island. On return to 'Roosy Roads', the film was quickly unloaded and processed for the high priority mission. Project *Volcano* was underway. Another RA-5C followed the next day, and for the next three weeks flight crews rotated through, and a detachment of maintenance personnel took care of two RA-5Cs. A highly rated scientist from the US Coast and Geodetic Survey was on hand to analyse the data they brought back.

A tholoidal plug of hot lava the size of a football field was rising through the crater lake in the mountain, which had been quiescent for 100 years. The lake had turned from a benign blue to an ugly, boiling pea-green.

Twice a day a Vigilante would launch and fly down to the volcano. The old crater was irregularly shaped, with one edge much higher than the other. A tropical cloud usually sat over the high ridge. The tactic the crews worked out was to fly low over the Caribbean and accelerate in afterburner to just under Mach one, fly up the 3000 ft mountain slope 100 ft over the lush greenery, push forward on the stick and go zero-G to level flight. While the RAN monitored cameras and IR, the pilot stared at a wall of solid rock coming at his nose at 300 knots. When the RAN called 'Nadir!', the pilot pulled up at 4 Gs and went on instruments into the cloud. Once clear, they came around for another run, until after four to six such runs low fuel forced them to go back to 'Roosy Roads'.

If the volcano began erupting and spewing rocks or lava, the damage would have as bad as AAA or SAM. Although the lava plug rose at better than eight inches a day at the start, it slowed, and after three weeks the project was called off. As the flight crews said, 'If Soufriere had erupted, we'd all be famous . . . but it didn't'.

1972 – SNAREs and 'Bears'

Long range bombers of the Soviet Union regularly attempted to locate and fly over US aircraft carriers throughout the Cold War. Fighters would be launched to intercept and then fly alongside the snoopers to block their view of the carrier task force. When the F-4 came into use, the back-seater was given a hand-held camera to take pictures. The results did not provide enough detail to analyse antennas, panels, weapons and other items of interest on the big Tupolevs and Ilyushins, so the RA-5Cs went along to use their sensors and high-resolution cameras, with the PECM bringing back usable data as well. IR was attempted, but flying directly overhead was too risky in the confrontational arena of fly-overs and intercepts.

In 1971, the use of airborne lasers had increased to the point where two Vigilantes of RVAH-12 (BuNos 148933 and 151727) were fitted with articulated, IR spectrum sensors. Known as SNARE, the classified equipment was mounted in a ten-inch tall turret that was hydraulically powered and aimed by the RAN through a viewfinder. The system had its own electronics, and recorded data on 16 channel tape.

RVAH-12 was chosen to employ the system because the squadron was scheduled to embark in *Independence*, which was in turn headed for a major NATO exercise in the far North Atlantic, close to the Arctic Circle. The goal of SNARE was to collect data about laser emitters and other related systems from the specially equipped

The National Museum of Naval Aviation's RA-5C BuNo 156624 intercepts a Soviet Tupolev Tu-95 'Bear' over the Pacific Ocean. In 1971, RVAH-12 was given two special installations called SNARE for the purpose of intercepts of laser equipped Soviet aircraft operating in the far north Atlantic (*Powell*)

Soviet 'Badger', 'Bear' and 'Bison' aircraft flying from airfields in the Murmansk area seeking out the *Independence* Battle Group. On completion of the cold weather operations, RVAH 12 was happy to spend the remaining months of its deployment in the Mediterranean.

An RVAH-14 RA-5C, complete with a flasher pod, flies over NAS Albany and the Flint River in 1968. RVAH-14 made three consecutive cruises on USS *John F Kennedy* (CVA-67) to the Mediterranean, followed by a fourth, and last, one on *Independence*. RVAH-14 was the last Vigilante squadron to be commissioned and first disestablished. Ron Pollard was with the 'Eagle Eyes' during both the Six Day and Yom Kippur Arab-Israeli wars. Albany's long runway had an alert pad from its days as Turner AFB. B-52s and KC-135s continued to use the alert area while Albany was a naval air station. This photograph was used on the cover of the Albany, Georgia, telephone directory (*EBAL*)

1973 – Yom Kippur War

After his 1967 Mediterranean deployment, which included the Six Day War, Ron Pollard stayed in RVAH-5 and went to Vietnam on *Constellation*. Following a tour instructing in the 'Recce RAG', he found himself involved in another Arab-Israeli war in October 1973, this time as CO of RVAH-14 flying from USS *Independence*;

'I was sent on a PECM flight covering the coast of Israel and the belligerent countries to the east. We were so intrigued with the excellent hits (on the RHAW indicators) we were getting, I stayed on track a little too long and realised I was not going to make my Charlie (landing) time. I had plenty of gas, so I went into max afterburner to the delight of the air controllers on the ship, who computed my speed off the radar. As I approached the "Indy", I noted the recovery was over, but the ship was still into the wind. I was cleared straight-in and I kept thinking, "I'd better not bolter". I didn't.

'The PECM data showed the Israeli Hawk batteries moving on the counter-offensive. That flight was the first indication that the Israeli Army had commenced their famous, and successful, counterattack. The attack guys didn't get to do anything, but we recce types sure stayed busy. The Yom Kippur War was followed by the OPEC oil embargo, and tensions in the eastern Med stayed high.'

1974 – Cyprus

In 1974, the *Forrestal* had the perfect schedule for a Mediterranean cruise – periods of good flying, punctuated by visits to the best ports in Europe. The idyll ended after four months when Turkey sent troops into Cyprus to bolster the Turkish portion of the divided island nation. War with Greece was imminent.

Forrestal was in port in Naples, Italy, with other ships of its task group when the recall came. The ships made an emergency sortie, leaving thousands of sailors and officers behind. It was a major operation to get them back to their ships, now patrolling off of Cyprus.

Allowing CVW-7 to fly normally was considered too sensitive, but NATO and United Nations

Cdr Ron Pollard poses with his named RA-5C prior to leading his unit, RVAH-14, on its final deployment in June 1973 (*Mersky*)

commanders needed to know the extent of the Turkish build-up, and the Greek response. Consequently, three times a day, *Forrestal* would launch three aircraft to search the surrounding seas. First off the catapult was the E-2 Hawkeye, with its immense radar and capability to search hundreds of miles of ocean. Next was an A-7 tanker (the A-6s were temporarily grounded), followed by the 'star of the show', a Vigilante from RVAH-6.

Normally the RA-5C would do its own search, but there was so much shipping in that part of the Mediterranean that it was more efficient for the E-2 to vector the aircraft from ship to ship. The Vigilante would top-off its fuel, drop to 200 ft and fly from vessel to vessel, adjusting its flyby heading for optimum light and camera angles. Between the systems on the Hawkeye and the Vigilante, accurate positions, courses and speeds were plotted for the surface contacts. Two to two-and-a-half hours later, the aircraft would land. Twenty minutes after that, photographs with enough detail to determine ships' names and identify cargo came out of the IOIC and into the hands of the commanders.

After more than a week of this schedule, the rest of the air wing was permitted to fly – albeit in an ever restricted amount of airspace. A month after the emergency sortie *Forrestal* returned to Naples for a few days and then went back to Cyprus, all hopes of sunny beaches and sightseeing forgotten. After another month at sea, the crisis had quietened down and RVAH-6 rode across the Atlantic and flew off into NAS Key West.

This photograph of *Forrestal's* flight deck was taken during the Cyprus Crisis of 1974. Three RVAH-6 Vigilantes sit side-by-side immediately aft of the carrier's island superstructure. AA 603 has its refuelling probe extended while its pilot runs through his preflight checks. In the background is an unmanned A-6 and two A-7s that are also preparing to launch – the latter may be acting as tankers for the RA-5C (*EBAL*)

1975 – Saigon evacuation

1975 was a grim year for the United States. The Viet Minh were victorious in Vietnam, the Khmer Rouge had taken over Cambodia and the Pathet Lao had risen to power in Laos. The dominoes had fallen.

The Cambodians had hijacked the freighter SS *Mayaguez* and run it ashore on a coastal island. The rescue of its crew was nearly a disaster, but the Navy was not called in.

Saigon itself, soon to be renamed Ho Chi Minh City, fell in April. The only Vigilante squadron in the area was RVAH-12 on *Enterprise*. Reconnaissance was not required as the ship loaded evacuees on board. American involvement in Vietnam was over.

1979 – The End

On 27 September 1964, Lt(jg) Dave Sharp ejected from RVAH-7 A-5A BuNo 147863 while deployed on *Enterprise*. On 28 September 1979, 15 years and a day later, Cdr Tom Myers, CO of RVAH-7, read the orders disestablishing the 'Peacemakers'. The last of ten Vigilante squadrons was no more.

Dave Sharp had preceded Myers as CO of the unit. Sharp's career was typical of many who began in the Vigilante, and became stalwarts of the reconnaissance community. That he was in the first Vigilante unit, and almost its last commander, was appropriate.

An RA-5C is launched from a waist catapult. The television scanner beneath the nose is readily visible from this angle. Straight back from it is a small blade-antenna, and next to that the opening for the optical viewfinder (*EBAL*)

Sharp began as a BN in A3Ds in Sanford, and was selected to be in the first class to train in Vigilantes in VAH-3. He was assigned to VAH-7 and went around the world on *Enterprise*. The jet that he and Lt Cdr Tuttle ejected from was the 25th Vigilante built.

Cdr Ken Enney (later CO of the RAG and CRAW-1) talked junior officer Sharp into remaining in the Navy, and he deployed with RVAH-7 to *WestPac* in 1966. He attended Navy post-graduate school, before undertaking a third cruise in RVAH-7. Returning to the Vigilante community, now in Albany, Sharp joined RVAH-12 and made another cruise to *WestPac*, as well as one to the Mediterranean. A joint tour at the Command Center in Omaha and a session at the Naval War College preceded selection for command of an RVAH squadron. He was the XO/CO for RVAH-7's penultimate cruise. Dave Sharp turned RVAH-7 over to Cdr Tom Myers, who had briefly been CO of RVAH-9;

'During the party after the 'Hooters" change of command, I received two messages as skipper of my first command. The first was an official directive to disestablish RVAH-9 in three months. The second message was from the Enlisted Party, telling me they needed more beer. I'm not sure that the timing of the official message could have been any worse.

'So three months later Barry Gastrock, CO of RVAH-5, and I closed our squadrons down in a joint ceremony. After almost a year on CRAW-1 Staff, I assumed command of RVAH-7.

'Being the skipper of the last squadron was a wonderful experience, and I wouldn't have had it any other way. Everyone that loved the "Vigi" wanted to be in that last squadron, and wanted to make that last cruise. RVAH-1 left behind a fully up aircraft at Subic for us to rob parts off of during our deployment. It is the one that is still on a platform in front of the old admin building on the hill.

'Then going to Singapore for a port call, *Ranger* collided with an oil tanker during the night transit. So we went back to Subic, filled the bow with concrete and because of the damage, *Ranger* could not get enough speed to launch Vigilantes in low wind conditions and we off-loaded the entire squadron at Cubi Point. It was a beautiful way to end the life of the fastest, most beautiful aircraft that ever graced the skies of this world. We flew anywhere we wanted, any altitude we wanted, as fast as we wanted, taking movies and pictures of each other. I had a crew where morale was so high you could walk on it.

'The last day, we moved back aboard, the *Ranger* sailed and the jets all flew out and landed. I tried to get everyone a "last" something'.

Lt Cdr Paul Habel (a nugget in RVAH-11 during *Linebacker*) and Lt Larry Parr had the last trap, in BuNo 156615, and, as Habel jokes, that after one last bolter!

Cdr Myers and Lt Cdr McManamon were on the last catapult shot, in BuNo 156608, for the fly-off to San Diego on 21 September 1979. The three Vigilantes joined up and made a spectacular low pass, dumping in burner past *Ranger*, the first carrier to deploy with the RA-5C.

Bob Dean had reported to RVAH-3 in 1966, and had made deployments in RVAH-6 on *Ranger* and *Enterprise* in 1967 and 1968. He was the XO of RVAH-12 for *America's* second deployment to Vietnam in 1970, and CO of RVAH-12 on *Independence* to the Mediterranean. A tour in the Pentagon was as an Action Officer in the Joint Reconnaissance

The last jets of RVAH-7, which was in turn the fleet's last Vigilante squadron. The black noses were unique to the unit, and some claimed they were applied as a sign of mourning. NH 611 (BuNo 156615) takes credit for performing the last shipboard landing by a Vigilante when Lt Cdr Paul Habel and Lt Larry Parr trapped aboard *Ranger* on 17 August 1979

Center. Capt Dean became the last commodore of CRAW-1.

The last Vigilante flight was on 20 November 1979 from NAS Key West to NAS Memphis. BuNo 156608 made the flight with its landing gear down because there was no time to repair the hydraulics. Capt E O Williams had been in the second deployable RVAH unit, commanded RVAH-14 and the RAG, was next-to-last CO of CRAW-1 and was stationed in Memphis. He delayed his Navy retirement until the last Vigilante arrived.

Capt Dean was another of the originals who sustained the excellence of the recce community and had the unhappy task of officially ending the Vigilante programme at an empty NAS Key West on 7 January 1980.

AFTER THE END

What happened to Navy airborne recce when the RA-5C was retired?

The single-seat RF-8 Crusader soldiered on for a few more years, and a Marine Corps RF-4B Phantom II detachment made its first carrier deployment. However, the major effort fell to the F-14 Tomcat. Much effort went into developing a pod that could be carried on the jet's weapons rack, and remain steady enough for high resolution photography. One fighter unit in each air wing would have three TARPS (Tactical Airborne Reconnaissance Pod System) for the additional role of reconnaissance. Despite the best efforts of personnel from former RVAH units, TARPS was never as effective as the RA-5C. Reconnaissance was a secondary mission, and it was treated as such. A new Shared Reconnaissance Pod (SHARP) is now entering service with the F/A-18F.

Times are still changing and technology constantly improving. Satellites that provide real-time IR, ultra-violet, radar or plain old visual imagery are in use. Unmanned aerial vehicles now go into high-threat areas without risking human operators. The suite of sensors available to battle commanders is at a level unheard of when the RA-5C Vigilante represented the latest in reconnaissance.

The RA-5C may prove to be the best reconnaissance aircraft ever built despite the high-tech vehicles coming into use. There is nothing comparable to well-trained, highly-motivated, professional and courageous pilots and RANs making decisions on the spot to collect the information needed by battlefield commanders.

'Vigis' that are no more. Photographed at the Davis-Monthan AFB 'boneyard' in 1973, these older model Vigilantes had been replaced in the fleet by new '156 series' aircraft. From the front to the rear, the squadrons represented in this photograph are RVAH-12, -3, -13 and -7, as well as two plain tails. All these were shown as 'stricken', i.e., scrapped, in May 1978 (*EBAL*)

APPENDICES

APPENDIX A

US NAVY AIRCRAFT DESIGNATIONS

The aircraft designations used in this book are the old, traditional US Navy system and the post-1962 unified system, as appropriate. Aeroplanes in the transition period are indicated in old/unified style, e.g. A3J-2/A-5B.

Traditional designations comprised a letter for the primary mission, a number showing how many of the type the company had made (1 was not shown) and a letter indicating the manufacturer. Dash numbers indicated model variants, while various prefix and suffix letters denoted specialised missions under the general category.

North American Aviation's letter was J (N was the Navy's own aircraft factory), so the first attack aircraft the company built was the AJ Savage. There was a turbo-prop version of the Savage designated A2J, so consequently the Vigilante began life as the A3J.

Similarly, and logically, D was Douglas' letter, and its Skyraider was the AD. A turbo-prop version (the Skyshark) was developed, and it became the A2D. Douglas' third attack aircraft was the A3D Skywarrior. Thus, in 1962, there were two A3s (this supposedly so confused then Secretary of Defense Robert McNamara that he insisted on the unified system). The Skywarrior remained the A-3 and the Vigilante became the A-5 (note the hyphens).

APPENDIX B

VIGILANTE DESIGNATIONS:

YA3J – Vigilante prototype. Two built (for some reason there was not a XA3J). First flight 31 August 1958.

A3J-1/A-5A – Bomber only. Issued to squadrons VAH-1, -3 and -7. Production ended in 1963.

A3J-2/A-5B – Raised fuselage for increased fuel capacity, altered engine intake ducts for higher thrust, modified wing structure to install four pylons for weapons or fuel tanks and modified BLC to blow from leading edge of wing for improved slow speed handling. Only two delivered to the Navy (VAH-3), with the others on the production line being modified into RA-5Cs.

RA-5C – A-5B converted to a reconnaissance platform through the addition of a belly 'canoe' containing interchangeable sensors and side-looking radar. A total of 43 new RA-5Cs were built, and all 18 B-models, plus 43 A-models, were converted to this standard in the NAR Columbus, Ohio, factory. Powered by J79-GE-8 engines.

'156 series' (RA-5D) – Because of the escalation of the war in Vietnam, 36 new Vigilantes were authorised in 1968. Powered by higher thrust J79-GE-10 engines, the aircraft boasted an improved airframe with redesigned intakes and a strake to the leading edge of the wing from the intake duct. The aircraft should have been designated RA-5Ds, but the politics of procurement and budget being what they are, the new airframes remained RA-5Cs. To differentiate between old and new aircraft, the final Vigilantes were referred to as '156 series' after their Navy bureau numbers.

Strakes, but not '156' – Airframe Change 328 allowed the J79-GE-10 to be installed. The modification was done during aircraft rework after 1974 on some pre-'156 series' RA-5Cs at the Jacksonville Overhaul Facility. RVAH-7 and -9 operated BuNos 146702, 149298, 149299 and 150831. There may have been more.

APPENDIX C

US NAVY SQUADRONS

US Navy squadrons with fixed-wing aircraft are designated V (H is for rotary-wing and Z was for lighter-than-air blimps and zeppelins), with the second letter indicating the squadron's primary mission, followed by a number. Many squadrons that flew Vigilantes trace their lineage to the VC (C for Composite, multi-role) squadrons flying AJ Savages. With the advent of the A3D/A-3 Skywarrior in the attack role, and because of the size of the aeroplane and its weapon, the squadrons became VAH (A for Attack, H for Heavy). Initially the Vigilante maintained the attack role as well as its new reconnaissance mission, and the squadrons were redesignated RVAH.

APPENDIX D

HOMES OF THE RECCE COMMUNITY

The official command structure of the Vigilante community was nine deployable fleet squadrons (RVAH-1, -5, -6, -7, -9, -11, -12, -13 and -14) and three training organisations – RVAH-3 was the replacement training squadron for pilots, RANs and maintenance men, the Naval Air Maintenance Training Detachment (NAMTraDet) taught specifics of mechanical, hydraulic, electric and electronic systems, and NIPSTraFac (Naval Intelligence Processing System Training Facility) supported RAG training missions and fleet squadrons while ashore, and taught the intelligence officers and photo specialists. These were all under the command of Commander Reconnaissance Attack Wing One (CRAW-1). Although the Vigilante squadrons, and their supporting units, were organised in a typical military chain of command, the term 'community' was appropriate.

At the height of RVAH manning in 1968, there were, at any given time, around 75 pilots in the world capable and current in landing an RA-5C on a ship. There was a slightly larger number of RANs. Not a large group, especially when compared with the Phantom II fighter force, which had almost 700 current pilots and a like number of RIOs. An RVAH squadron had all the jobs every other Navy unit had, but only half the officers to perform them.

Additionally, the A-4, A-6, F-8 and F-4 squadrons were divided between the East and West Coasts. The Vigilantes were always at a single base. Rotating between sea duty in one of the nine squadrons and shore duty, instructing in the RAG or on the CRAW-1 staff, and then back to sea duty in the Vigilante made for a familiarity which carried over into the families of the men as well. It was a small world where reputation was important. Word of crashes and mishaps spread fast. Personal support from friends, neighbours and squadron mates was always near.

The Vigilante community evolved out of the heavy attack community which had started life in Sanford, Florida. The base had been a Navy training station during World War 2, firstly for fighters and later for the PV Ventura medium bomber. Sanford was closed at the end of the war. In the late 1950s, and with the start of the Navy's Heavy Attack programme, NAS Sanford was recommissioned.

The first VAH squadrons operated P2V Neptune and AJ Savage aircraft there as part of HatWing 1. The VAH squadrons transitioned to the A3D/A-3 Skywarrior and called NAS Sanford their home base while deploying on aircraft carriers. The first A3J/A-5 Vigilantes arrived for replacement training squadron VAH-3 in June, 1961. Soon after, replacement squadrons were reorganised, with VAH-123 at NAS Whidbey Island, Washington, doing all the Skywarrior training and VAH-3 becoming the single site for Vigilantes.

The advent of the RA-5C induced a spate of redesignations to recognise the reconnaissance mission. VAH-3 remained the RAG, but became RVAH-3 in

July 1964. The controlling commodore changed to Reconnaissance Attack Wing One (CRAW-1), and as each squadron transitioned to the RA-5C, their designation went from VAH to RVAH.

The USAF was closing Turner AFB in Albany, Georgia – Gary Powers, the U-2 pilot shot down over the Soviet Union, had been recruited while assigned to Turner AFB. Richard Russell of Georgia was the new head of the Senate Armed Services Committee, and he was not about to let his state lose a major base, and he convinced the Navy to move CRAW-1 and all the RVAH squadrons to Albany. RVAH-3 made the move in May 1968. RVAH-11, -13, -6 and -1 were deployed from Sanford, and they duly returned to what was now NAS Albany.

The move initially resulted in family separations, financial losses on home sales and general havoc. That the base was inland did not particularly affect operations as the squadrons had to fly to either coast to work with their assigned aircraft carriers anyway. Step by step, Albany became an efficient and comfortable base for the 'Vigi' community. Life in the small city was good. One pilot's wife described it as, 'Warm, wacky and wonderful. A surprisingly intellectual and friendly town. The whole community arrived in a group and we made our own fun as we got to know our civilian neighbours'. Then Senator Russell died.

The new chairman of the Armed Services Committee cut a deal, and since the Navy no longer had ships, submarines or aviation squadrons in Key West, another move for the Vigilante community was decreed. Some families moved six months in advance to be sure of getting a house on base, as places to live in the small vacation city were expensive and hard to find. RVAH-3 officially shifted to Key West in January 1973. Again, deployed squadrons left from one base and came back months later to another. For the officers and sailors, life as a 'Conch' (a resident of the Florida Keys) could not have been more of a change from the grey steel, noise and bustle of shipboard life.

NAS Key West (the airfield is actually on Boca Chica) remained the home of the Vigilantes until the last squadrons were disestablished in late1979.

APPENDIX E

SURVIVING VIGILANTES

BuNo 156624 (NAA103) was part of a 'matched set' when new, and assigned to RVAH-6. BuNos 156623, 24, 25, 26 and 27 were NH 601, 602, 603, 604 and 605 respectively during the 1970-71 deployment on *Kitty Hawk*. BuNo 156624 remained with RVAH-6 for the 1972 *America* cruise, before going to RVAH-5 and returning to RVAH-6 for the 'Fleur's' final deployment. BuNo 156624 is on display at the National Museum of Naval Aviation at NAS Pensacola, Florida, in the 1978 markings of RVAH-6.

BuNo 156608 (NAA 67) was the first of the 'supplemental buy' Vigilantes and, appropriately, the last operational RA-5C. It served with RVAH-5 and the 'Recce RAG', before garnering a string of 'lasts' with RVAH-7 – the last catapult shot in the last squadron on the last deployment. The jet's last flight was to NAS Memphis, Tennessee, where it is on display marked up in its final paint scheme with RVAH-7 .

BuNo 146697 (NAA 6) is the only surviving A3J, and one of two Vigilantes on display at NAS Patuxent River, Maryland.

BuNo 156643 (NAA122) was the last Vigilante built, and is an exhibit at the Patuxent River Naval Air Test and Evaluation Museum. It served in RVAH-9 and -12, and performed Automatic Carrier Landing System (ACLS) certification on aircraft carriers for the Naval Air Test Center. The Vigilante wears the paint scheme of the NATC Flight Test Division in the mid 1970s.

BuNo 149289 (NAA 49/C53) is an A-5A conversion. The Vigilante is just one of a number of military aircraft saved from destruction because of the proximity of the Pima Air Museum in Tucson, Arizona, to the Military Aircraft Storage and Disposal Center (MASDC) at nearby Davis-Monthan AFB. The Pima museum was formed to give the public a closer look at examples of the thousands of aircraft in storage or awaiting disposal at MASDC. BuNo 149289 has been preserved in the colours of RVAH-3, as indeed are most other Vigilantes on display today. Since all Vigilante crew members and maintainers went through the 'Recce RAG', RVAH-3's orange stripes are a way to avoid showing favouritism!

BuNo 151629 (NAA 35) was condemned to the Davis-Monthan 'boneyard', but was spared to go on display in the museum within the grounds of the Pueblo Memorial Airport in Colorado. It is presently on display in RVAH-3 markings.

BuNo 156621 (NAA100) was originally on display at NAS Pensacola, but it was moved to the Intrepid Air-Space Museum floating on the East River in New York City. Also painted in RVAH-3 markings, BuNo 156621 shares space on the flight deck of USS *Intrepid* (CVS-11) with other aeroplanes that never actually operated from the veteran carrier when it was in fleet service.

BuNo 156612 (NAA 91) participated in RVAH-12's last deployment, and then flew in the last days of the 'Recce RAG'. It is on display at the main gate of the Vigilante's final base at NAS Key West, Florida, still in the orange lightning bolt markings of RVAH-3. Two RA-5C pilots and two RANs who live in the Florida Keys have their names painted beneath the cockpits – Art Skelly, John Smittle, Randy McDonald and Mike Bankester.

BuNo 156632 (NAA111) was one of the many Vigilantes taken to the Naval Weapons Center (NWC) at China Lake, in California, for use as a target and for weapons testing. However, before it could be shot at, the aircraft was trucked to Sanford, Florida, where it was restored and put on display at Sanford Airport in May 2003. The airport is the former NAS Sanford, where the Vigilante community had its start. The aircraft wears the colours of RVAH-3, which was based at Sanford from 1963 to 1968.

BuNo 156638 (NAA117) is another RA-5C saved from the NWC China Lake firing ranges. Still marked in the red, white and blue of its last squadron, RVAH-12, BuNo 156638 is on display at NAS Fallon, Nevada.

BuNo 156627 (NAA106) made at least two deployments in RVAH-6 following its delivery to the unit from the North American factory. RVAH-1, on its last cruise, left the perfectly serviceable Vigilante at Cubi Point, in the Philippines, for RVAH-7 to fly before it also went home. Towed to 'the top of the hill', the aircraft remains in the open, but after the US Navy left the base in 1991, a local art school was turned loose and BuNo 156627 bears an overall psychedelic swirl of bright paint!

BuNo 146698 (NAA 7/C69) was flown into the Naval Air Engineering Center at Lakehurst, New Jersey, to be used for testing catapults and arresting gear. Once out of date, it was abandoned in a field until in 1982 the Aviation Boatswainmate School restored the Vigilante sufficiently to display it on the main road through the base. The Navy gave several aeroplanes to the new Air Victory Museum in Millville, New Jersey in the early 1990s. When asked what the current status of the Vigilante was, the museum's curator wrote, 'I'm sorry to tell you that the RA-5C, BuNo 146698, was destroyed in transit from Lakehurst to the Air Victory Museum. It had started an uncontrollable gyration under the CH-47 transport helicopter and had to be cut loose. The aircraft was a total loss. I wish that we still had the "Vigi", but alas it is no more.'

BuNo 151727 (NAA 42) and **BuNo 156610** (NAA 89) are listed as having been stricken at Rota, in Spain. Although there were rumours that one of them was on display, their status is undetermined.

BuNo 156622 (NAA101), **BuNo 156625** (NAA104), **BuNo 156628** (NAA107), and **BuNo 156636** (NAA115) are listed as in storage, vice stricken, at Davis-Monthan AFB, so they may yet have a chance to become museum pieces sometime in the future.

APPENDIX F

RVAH SQUADRONS

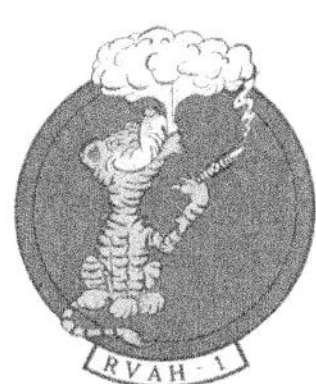

RVAH-1 began in November 1965 as VAH-1, having previously been the first squadron to fly A-3 Skywarriors. When an inter-squadron design contest produced no winner for a new unit emblem, several junior officer BNs were sent to a cartoonists convention in Jacksonville and came back with the emblem of the grinning tiger blowing a nuclear cloud.
Call-sign: 'Comanche Trail'
Nickname: 'Smoking Tigers'

RVAH-3 began as VAH-3 in Jacksonville in 1956, and deployed to the Mediterranean, before moving to Sanford and becoming the replacement training squadron. RVAH-3 flew more types of aircraft than any other RAG. Besides a dozen Vigilantes, there were four TA-3B Skywarriors, with the bomb-bays set up with extra seats and radar scopes for training BN/RANs, four TA-4J Skyhawks to chase RA-5C flights and keep pilots proficient and a single old C-117D Skytrain that was gainfully employed as a utility transport. The unit's distinctive crest was the result of an inter-squadron design contest.
Call-sign: 'Drake'
Nicknames: 'Recce RAG', 'Dragons'

RVAH-5 traced its history to VC-5 in 1948, when the squadron flew P2V Neptunes as bombers, before it became the first squadron to operate AJ Savages. Looking for a name, the crews came up with 'The Savage Sons of Sanford' – a pun on the aircraft, and where they were based. The name and number remained through A3D Skywarriors as VAH-5 and RA-5C Vigilantes as RVAH-5, although after moving to NAS Albany the 'of Sanford' was dropped. The origin of the 'Mushmouth' cartoon of a cannibal as an emblem and nickname remains somewhat obscure. Display of the 'Mushmouth' came and went with the tides of political correctness.
Call-sign: 'Old Kentucky'
Nicknames: 'Mushmouths', 'Savage Sons'

RVAH-6 was formed with a mix of P2V Neptunes and AJ Savages in 1950 as VC-6. The heraldic symbol for the sixth Vigilante unit is the *Fleur-de-lis*. The trident symbolises sea power and the Omega represents the ultimate. Being called the 'Fleurs' was acceptable, but calling RVAH-6 the 'Flowers of the Fleet' when near serving members of the squadron was risky!
Call-sign: 'Fieldgoal'
Nickname: 'Fleurs'
Motto: *Celeritas cum Accurate* (Speed with Accuracy)

RVAH-7 dates back to VC-7, established in California in 1950. VAH-7 moved with its AJ Savages to Sanford, where it flew A3Ds before becoming the first Vigilante squadron. The 'Peacemakers' were also the last Vigilante squadron. The badge using the cocked six-guns and halo of seven stars came into use when the squadron received the first fleet Vigilantes.
Call-sign: 'Flare'
Nickname: 'Peacemakers'

RVAH-9 was established as VC-9, and it flew both TBM Avengers left over from World War 2 and P2V Neptunes. When equipped with the AJ Savage, VC/VAH-9 conducted some of the earliest air refuellings. The Owl emblem is a variation on an earlier one which had a Hooter Owl with a bomb burst behind it.
Call-sign: 'Hooter'
Nickname: 'Hooters'

RVAH-11 also began as a VC squadron with P2Vs and AJs. As VAH-11, it completed six deployments with A3D Skywarriors, before transitioning to the RA-5C. The original emblem had a checkered flood covering the globe, and the A3Ds were decorated with check-patterned bands, leading to the nick-name 'Checkertails'. The emblem was changed with assumption of the reconnaissance mission.
Call-sign: 'Glen Rock'
Nickname: 'Checkertails'

RVAH-12 was the first squadron to be specifically established as an RVAH with RA-5Cs. The Roman XII is framed by a spear at supersonic speed.
Call-sign: 'Speartip'
Nickname: 'Tips'
Motto: We Point the Way.

RVAH-13 was established with A-3s in Sanford in 1961. Like other Navy squadrons, VAH-13 looked to alcohol for inspiration for its squadron emblem (the boar's head for the VF-11 'Red Rippers' is from a Gordon's gin bottle, VA-212's rampant lion was from Löwenbräu beer and VA-37's blue bull from a popular malt beverage). Heavy Attack Squadron Thirteen chose the spread-winged bat which graced bottles of Bacardi rum (the rumour was that the company sent the unit a case of its product every Christmas). The emblem remained unchanged when A-3 Skywarriors were exchanged for RA-5C Vigilantes in 1964.
Call-sign: 'Flint River'
Nickname: 'Bats'

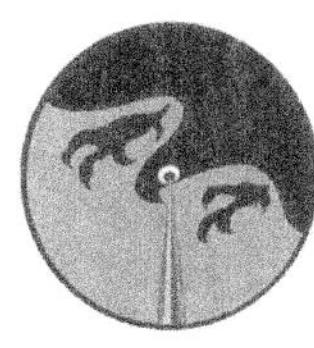

RVAH-14 was the other squadron established as an RVAH. It was also the shortest lived of the Vigilante squadrons, being established in February 1968 and stood down May 1974 after completing four deployments. RVAH-14 was the only frontline Vigilante unit not to see action in Vietnam. Its emblem was designed by Roy Crane, the creator of the *Buzz Sawyer* comic strip.
Call-sign: 'Eagle Eye'

APPENDIX G

VIGILANTE LOSS LIST (IN CHRONOLOGICAL ORDER)

YR/MO/DAY	BuNo	NAA NUMBER	ACTION/LOCATION	UNIT	CREW
Development/Test					
59/6/3	145158	2	Ejection Columbus, OH		Hopkins
61/3/17	146700	9	Ejection Patuxent River, MD		Lt Cdr Grimes
61/8/29	147855	17	Ejection NASWF, Albuquerque, NM		Gugenbiller, Lt Biehl
62/11/27	148927	29	Stricken Sanford, FL		
63/1/9	146694	3	Ejection Columbus, OH		Burdick
73/7/23	156637	116	Ejection Patuxent River, MD		Lt Cdr Hauck
Fleet					
62/1/9	147862	24	Stricken USS *Franklin D Roosevelt*	RVAH-3	Cdr Gear
62/11/27	148926	28/C78	Ejection Tokyo, Japan	RVAH-6	Lt Cdr Campbell, Lt Cook
63/2/20	149282	42	Stricken USS *Enterprise*	RVAH-7	Lt Kruse, Lt(jg) Cottle
63/9/19	149290	50	Stricken USS *Independence*	RVAH-1	Lt Cdr Conrey, Lt Garret
63/9/5	148930	32	Ejection Sanford, FL	RVAH-3	Lt Cdr Lovelace, ADJ-1 Kelsey
64/11/14	149308	68	Ejection Sanford, FL	RVAH-9	Lt Cdr Smith, ADJC Carolyers
64/12/23	151821	27	Ejection Sanford, FL	RVAH-13	Cdr Nolta, Lt(jg) Stokes
64/12/9	149306	66	Combat loss? USS *Ranger*	RVAH-5	Lt Cdr Beard, Lt(jg) Cronin
64/5/5	148931	33	Ejection USS *Enterprise*	RVAH-7	Lt Cdr Chapdelaine, AE1 Stringer
64/9/20	150828	6	Ejection USS *Saratoga*	RVAH-1	Lt Cdr Williams, Lt Haisten
64/9/27	147863	25	Ejection USS *Enterprise*	RVAH-7	Lt Cdr Tuttle, Lt(jg) Sharp
64/9/3	151616	22	Ejection in Sanford, FL	RVAH-1	Lt Cdr Bell, AMHC Pemberton
64/9/8	149292	52	Ejection in Sanford, FL	RVAH-3	Lt Cdr Moore, Lt(jg) Haney
65/7/20	151819	25	Lost at sea USS *Independence*	RVAH-1	Cdr Matula, Lt Gronquist
65/10/16	150836	14	Ejection USS *America*	RVAH-5	Lt Cdr Pippen, Lt(jg) Otis
65/10/16	151615	21	Combat loss USS *Independence*	RVAH-1	Lt Cdr Bell, Lt Cdr Hutton
65/10/17	150835	13	Ejection USS *America*	RVAH-5	Lt Pirrotte, Ens McClure
65/12/15	150827	5	Ejection Sanford, FL	RVAH-3	Cdr McLain, Lt Morgan
65/12/16	151633	39	Combat loss USS *Enterprise*	RVAH-7	Lt Sutor, Lt(jg) Dresser
65/12/20	151624	30	Combat loss USS *Kitty Hawk*	RVAH-13	Lt Cdr Johnson, Lt Cdr Nordahl
65/12/22	151632	38	Combat loss USS *Kitty Hawk*	RVAH-13	Lt Cdr Lukenbach, Lt Cdr Daigel
66/1/16	149312	72	Stricken USS *Ranger*	RVAH-9	Lt Cdr Schoonover, Ens Hollingsworth
66/2/3	151625	31	Combat loss USS Kitty Hawk	RVAH-13	Lt Coffee, Lt(jg) Hanson
66/5/21	149285	45/C45	Ejection USS *America*	RVAH-5	Lt Cdr Meyer, Lt(jg) Waggoner
66/8/19	149309	69	Combat loss USS *Constellation*	RVAH-6	Lt Cdr Thompson Lt(jg) Parten
66/10/6	149288	48/C65	Ejection USS Enterprise	RVAH-7	Lt Sutor, Lt(jg) Carrothers
66/10/23	150830	8	Combat loss USS *Constellation*	RVAH-6	Lt Cdr Kolstad, Lt(jg) Klennert
67/2/12	151623	29	Combat loss USS *Enterprise*	RVAH-7	Cdr Jarvis, Lt(jg) Artzlip
67/3/9	151627	33	Combat loss USS *Kitty Hawk*	RVAH-13	Cdr Putnam, Lt(jg) Prendergast
67/5/19	150826	4	Combat loss USS *Kitty Hawk*	RVAH-13	Cdr Griffen, Lt Walters
67/6/14	149314	74	Ejection Sanford, FL	RVAH-3	Lt Cdr Butler, Ens Smith
67/7/29	148932	34/C49	Stricken USS *Forrestal* (flight deck fire)	RVAH-11	
67/7/29	149284	44/C51	Stricken USS *Forrestal* (flight deck fire)	RVAH-11	
67/7/29	149305	65	Stricken USS *Forrestal* (flight deck fire)	RVAH-11	
67/8/13	151634	40	Combat loss USS *Constellation*	RVAH-12	Lt Cdr Hyatt, Lt(jg) Goodermote
67/8/17	149302	62	lost at sea, combat? USS *Constellation*	RVAH-12	Cdr Dixon, Lt(jg) Hom
67/10/3	149315	75	Ejection Sanford, FL	RVAH-3	Lt Cdr Scruggs
67/12/6	151728	43	Ejection Miami, FL	RVAH-3	Lt Cdr Sledge, Lt(jg) Lowrie
68/5/5	149278	38/C54	Combat loss USS *Enterprise*	RVAH-1	Lt Norrington, Lt Tangeman
68/5/14	147854	16/C84	Ejection USS *Independence*	RVAH-7	Cdr Pritscher, Lt(jg) Feldhaus
68/5/18	149283	43/C50	Combat loss USS *Kitty Hawk*	RVAH-11	Cdr James, Lt Cdr Monroe
68/9/9	149280	40/C46	Lost at sea USS *Ranger*	RVAH-3	Lt Cdr Woolf, Lt(jg) Kirby
68/10/25	151626	32	Stricken USS *Forrestal*	RVAH-12	
68/11/25	149293	53/C62	Combat loss USS *Constellation*	RVAH-5	Cdr Stamm, Lt(jg) Thum
69/2/19	151631	37	Ejection USS *John F Kennedy*	RVAH-14	Lt Cdr Bright, Lt(jg) Ellis
69/3/31	150842	20	Combat loss USS *Enterprise*	RVAH-6	Cdr White, Lt Carpenter
69/6/19	149287	471C59	Ejection Albany, GA	RVAH-7	Cdr Barnes, Lt(jg) Hornick
69/9/9	150833	11	Ejection USS *John F Kennedy*	RVAH-14	Lt Cdr Reed, Lt Marechal

70/1/1	148928	30/C78	Ejection Clark AFB, Philippines	RVAH-7	Cdr Billings (CAG 14), Lt(jg) Beaver
70/1/23	150825	3	Ejection USS *Forrestal*	RVAH-13	Cdr Barnes, Lt(jg) Wolfe
70/2/2	149316	76	Ejection USS *Forrestal*	RVAH-13	Lt Jenkins, Lt Standridge
70/3/5	151620	26	Ejection Albany, GA	RVAH-12	Cdr Huber
70/7/22	156611	90	Lost at sea USS *Independence*	RVAH-11	Lt Cdr Karr, Lt Cdr Pullinger
70/8/6	151817	23	Ejection USS *John F Kennedy*	RVAH-14	Cdr Williams, Lt Feeback
70/9/27	156629	108	Ejection USS *Ranger*	RVAH-1	Lt Cdr Renner, Lt Joseph
71/10/17	156634	113	Lost at sea USS *Enterprise*	RVAH-5	Cdr Everett, Lt Cdr Stokes
72/3/1	156630	109	Ejection Albany, GA	RVAH-1	Lt Pigeon, Lt Bixler
72/5/5	147850	12/C58	Ejection Albany, GA	RVAH-12	Cdr Bolte, Lt(jg) Hawken
72/5/7	151618	24	Combat loss USS *Kitty Hawk*	RVAH-7	Cdr Polfer, Lt(jg) Kernan
72/6/7	156616	95	Combat loss USS *Saratoga*	RVAH-1	Lt Cdr Smith, Lt Kunz
72/12/28	156633	112	Combat loss USS *Enterprise*	RVAH-13	Lt Cdr Agnew, Lt Haifley
73/5/21	156609	68	Ejection USS *Constellation*	RVAH-12	Lt Cdr Fowler, Lt(jg) Dipadova
74/3/5	149296	58/C77	Ejection at sea Key West, FL	RVAH-3	Lt Carson, Lt Cdr Comstock
74/7/11	156614	93	Ejection USS *Forrestal*	RVAH-6	Lt Rutledge, Lt(jg) Parr
74/8/13	151630	36	Ejection Naples, FL	RVAH-3	Lt Cdr McKay, Lt Stevens
75/2/2	156623	02	Lost at sea USS *Saratoga*	RVAH-11	Cdr Hogan, Lt Cdr Mullholland
78/1/12	156619	98	Ejection Albany, GA	RVAH-3	Lt Cdr Watt, Lt Cdr Criswell

Stricken on ship or NAS other than Jacksonville or Key West usually means that the aircraft was unrepairable as the result of an accident

Display

73/13/1	146697	6	Stricken, gate guard NAS Patuxent River, MD
75/7/31	146698	7/C69	Stricken Lakehurst, written off in helicopter drop
78/5/4	149289	49/C53	Davis-Monthan to Pima Museum, AZ
78/5/4	151629	35	Davis-Monthan to Pueblo, CO, museum
78/6/19	156612	91	Static display at NAS Key West, FL
78/10/11	156624	103	Static display at National Museum of Naval Aviation, Pensacola, FL
78/11/21	156621	100	From Pensacola to USS *Intrepid* museum, NY
79/3/26	156627	106	Stricken Cubi Point, Philippines
79/6/15	156643	122	Static display at NAS Patuxent River, MD
79/8/1	156638	117	NWC China Lake to NAS Fallon, NV
79/8/1	156632	111	NWC China Lake to Sanford, FL
79/11/20	156608	67	Static display at NAS Memphis, TN

NAS Disposal*

65/1/6	148924	26	Stricken Sanford
69/10/30	149303	63	Stricken?
71/12/13	147858	20/C64	Stricken Albany, GA
72/1/26	150837	15	Stricken Key West, FL
72/1/26	150841	19	Stricken Jacksonville, FL
72/1/26	151727	42	Stricken Rota, Spain
73/12/12	146695	41/C87	Stricken Key West, FL
75/1/3	149300	80	Stricken Jacksonville, FL
75/5/9	148929	31/C71	Stricken Jacksonville, FL
75/7/1	151622	28	Stricken Key West, FL
76/6/8	147853	15/C85	Stricken Jacksonville, FL
76/6/8	147856	18/C86	Stricken Jacksonville, FL
76/6/8	150823	1	Stricken Jacksonville, FL
76/7/31	149276	36/C52	Stricken Key West, FL
76/11/18	150824	2	Stricken Key West, FL
76/11/18	156617	96	Stricken Key West, FL
77/5/27	147860	22/C82	Stricken Key West, FL
77/9/20	149299	59/C75	Stricken Key West, FL
78/2/16	149301	81	Stricken Key West, FL
78/2/7	156635	114	Stricken Rota, Spain
78/6/19	156626	105	Stricken Key West, FL
78/10/31	156610	89	Stricken Rota, Spain
79/1/13	156620	99	Stricken North Island, CA
79/3/?	150831	9	Stricken Jacksonville, FL
81/1/11	147851	13	Stricken Patuxent River, Maryland

*BuNos not listed above stricken at MASDC Davis-Monthan AFB, AZ

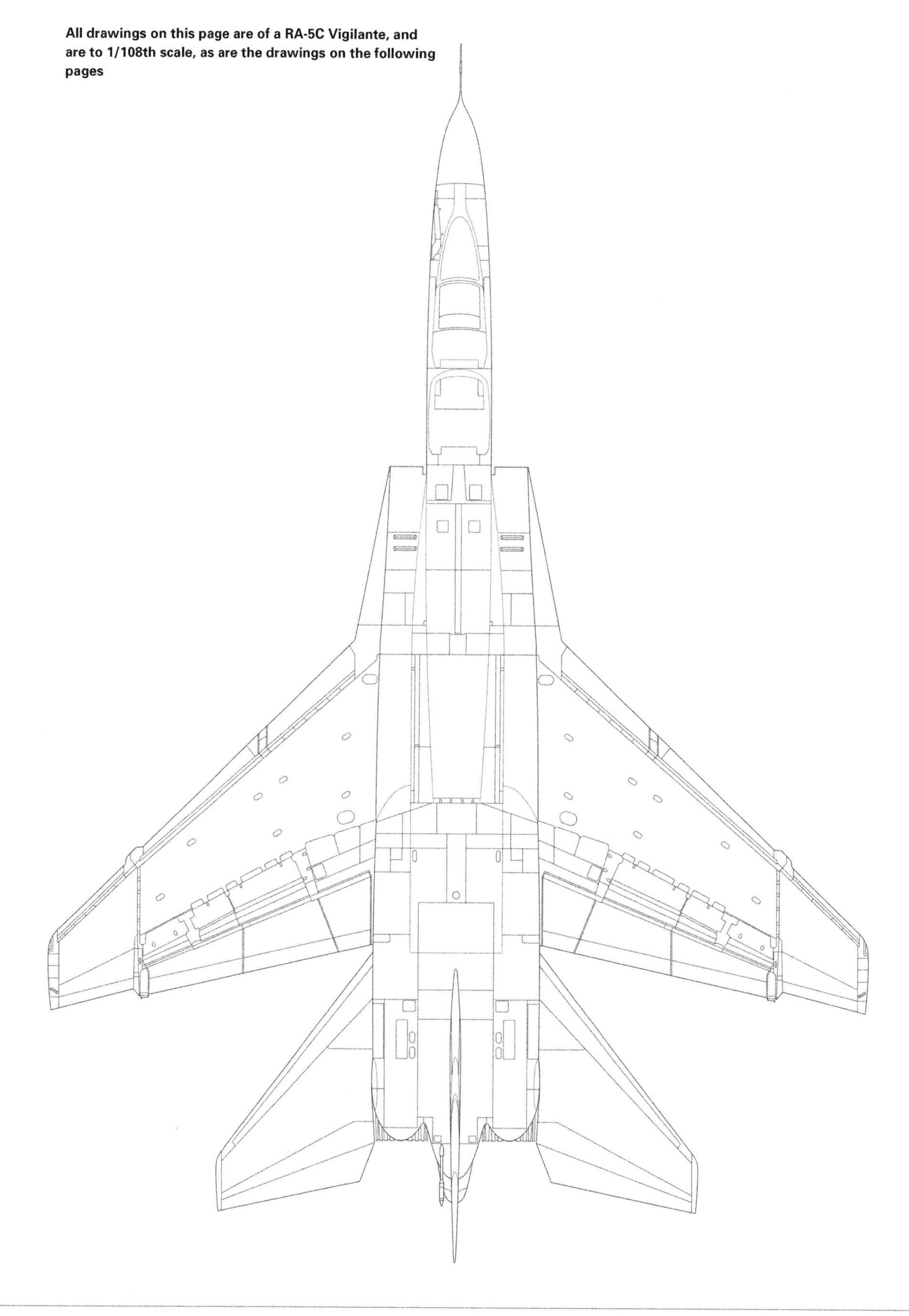

All drawings on this page are of a RA-5C Vigilante, and are to 1/108th scale, as are the drawings on the following pages

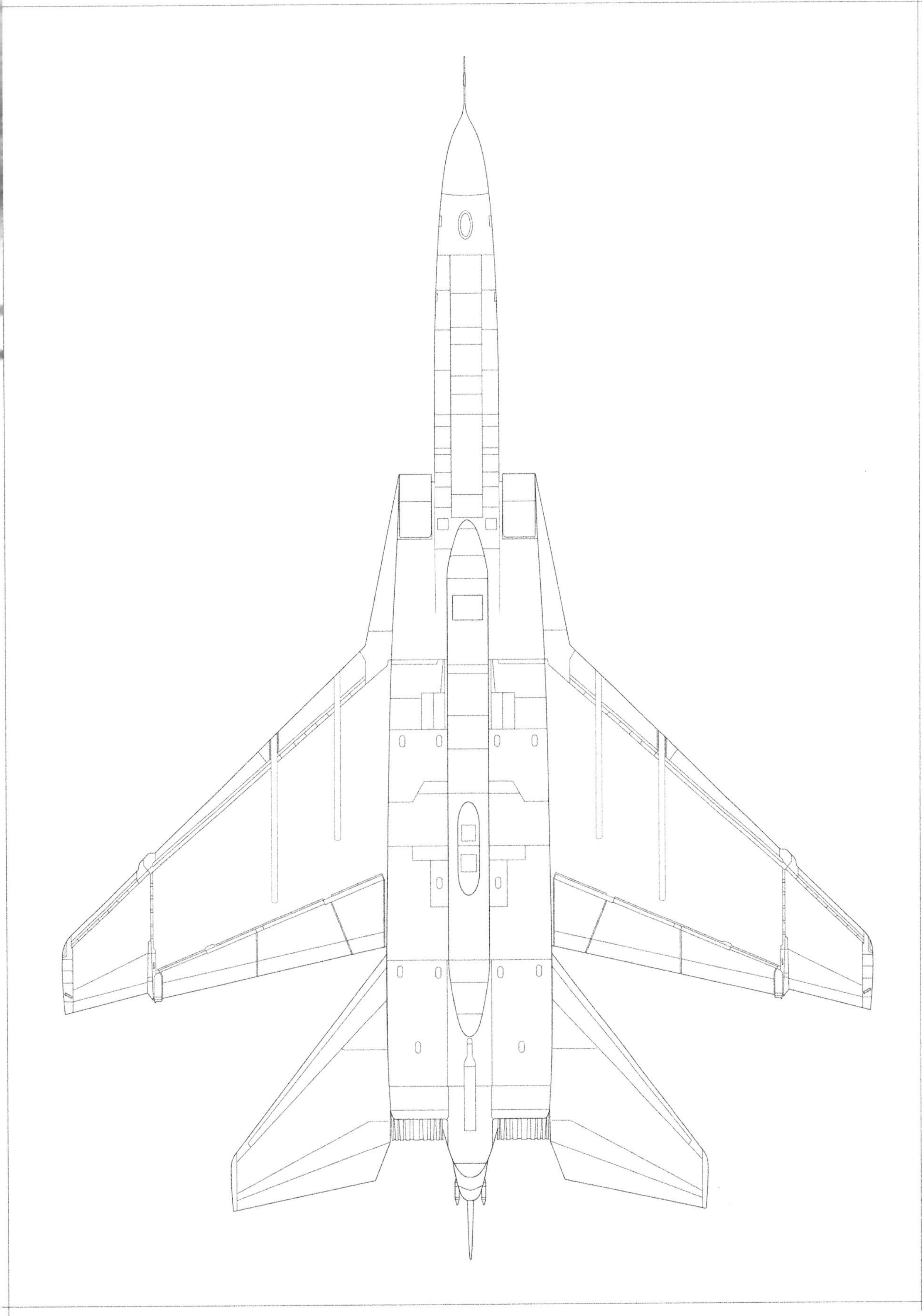

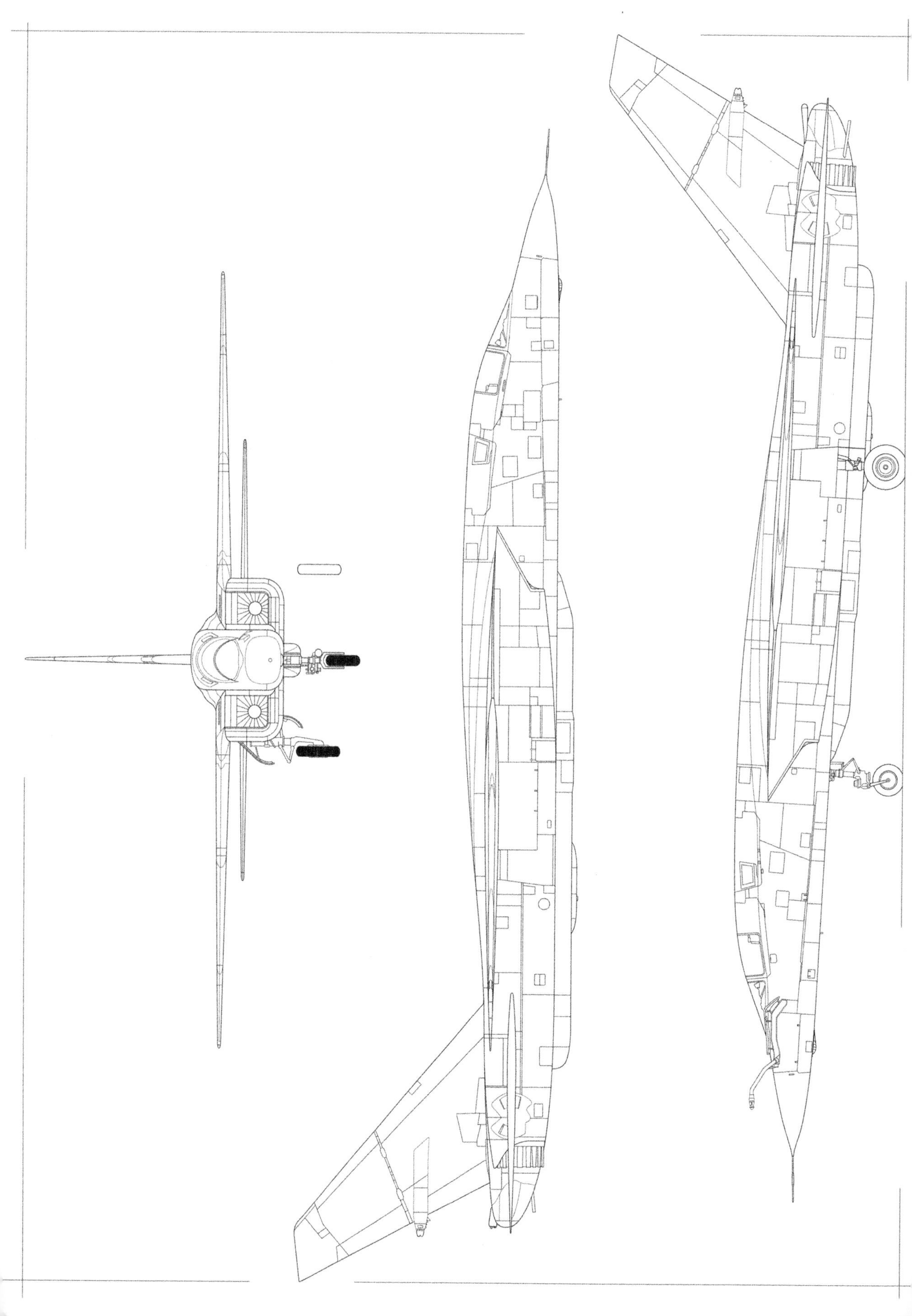

COLOUR PLATES

1
RA-5C BuNo 149312/NG 104 of RVAH-5/CVW-9, USS *Ranger*, December 1964
As the first squadron to deploy with the RA-5C, the 'Savage Sons of Sanford' had the difficult task of working with a new aeroplane and going into combat at the same time. The wavy grey-white demarcation, pale blue NAVY titling and small bureau number mark this as a Vigilante that was delivered fresh from the factory to RVAH-5. BuNo149312 was subsequently transferred to RVAH-9 and returned to *WestPac* aboard *Ranger* in December 1965. On 16 January 1966, during what should have been a routine carrier landing at the end of a reconnaissance mission, the jet's starboard engine exploded and the Vigilante crashed into the sea, with the loss of Lt Cdr Charles Schoonover and Ens Hal Hollingsworth.

2
RA-5C BuNo 151615/AG 601 of RVAH-1/CVW-7, USS *Independence*, 1965
Independence made only one deployment to *WestPac*. An Atlantic Fleet carrier, it was scheduled for a cruise in the Mediterranean when the situation in Vietnam worsened and the vessel was diverted to the Tonkin Gulf. The first carrier to operate A-6s, and with RA-5Cs embarked on only the type's second deployment, *Independence's* complement of factory 'tech reps' practically outnumbered the ship's company! RVAH-1 carried the unique shade of factory blue over to the nose modex and CVW-7 AG codes on its jets. The Vigilante is depicted in artwork carrying a flasher pod under its port wing. BuNo 151615 was the first RA-5C to be officially categorised as shot down in Vietnam when, on 16 October 1965, it was hit in the tail either by shrapnel from an exploding SA-2 or AAA while looking for SAM sites near Hon Gay. The flight controls failed and Lt Cdr James Bell, pilot, and Lt Cdr 'Duffy' Hutton, RAN, ejected. They were soon picked up by local fishermen and became PoWs.

3
RA-5C BuNo 151633/NG 102 of RVAH-7/CVW-9, USS *Enterprise*, December 1965
VAH-7 was the first Vigilante squadron, and it had deployed on *Enterprise* with A3Js in 1962-63. The unit made the transition to the RA-5C and stayed with CVAN-65 on its next cruise. By now the jet's factory blue markings have gone, and the demarcation line has straightened out during the the course of routine maintenance. BuNo 151633 was lost over the far west coast of South Vietnam on 16 December 1965. Pilot, Lt J K Sutor, and RAN, Lt(jg) G B Dresser, ejected and were rescued by a US Army UH-1B Huey helicopter, which hovered with its landing-skid on the water in order to pick them up.

4
RA-5C BuNo 151632/NH 603 of RVAH-13/CVW-11, USS *Kitty Hawk*, December 1965
The 'Bats' of RVAH-13 kept the Oriental-style tail codes during all their deployments. The unit would lose more Vigilantes in combat than any other RVAH squadron. In 1966-67, RVAH-13 lost three jets, including BuNo 151632. On 22 December 1965, 'Flint River 603' was on a pre-strike photography mission to Hai Duong when RAN, Lt(jg) Glenn Daigle, felt the Vigilante take a hit and he could not talk to his pilot, Lt Cdr Max Lukenbach – Daigle had to assume that the latter was either unconscious or dead. Seconds later there was an explosion, and the RAN was ejected from his cockpit. Daigle does not remember pulling the face-curtain or the alternate ejection handles. He became a PoW, and was released in February 1973.

5
RA-5C BuNo 148933/NK 904 of RVAH-9/CVW-14, USS *Ranger*, 1966
The black tail code on the dark green tail band made it difficult to read the air wing identifier on 'Hooter' Vigilantes. The RA-5C had retractable, red rotating beacons on the top and bottom of the fuselage. Required for normal flying, they were turned off/retracted in a hostile area. BuNo 148933 was modified to carry the SNARE special IR sensor turret while assigned to RVAH-12 in 1972.

6
RA-5C BuNo 149309/NL 703 of RVAH-6/CVW-15, USS *Constellation*, 19 August 1966
For their first RA-5C cruise, the 'Fleurs' added the speed-slash with *fleur-de-lis* that the squadron had carried on its A3D Skywarriors with when they were VAH-6. On 19 August 1966, BuNo 149309 was hit by AAA during a road reconnaissance mission northwest of Vinh, the jet immediately rolling inverted, out of control. Lt Cdr Jim Thompson and his RAN, Lt(jg) G Parten, ejected while still flying at supersonic speed. Both men were rescued from the sea.

7
RA-5C BuNo 151727/NH 606 of RVAH-13/CVW-11, USS *Kitty Hawk*, late 1966
One of several camouflage schemes attempted when MiGs seemed to be the primary threat, the Vigilantes, and other fast jet types in CVW-11, were repainted after ground fire proved more hazardous. The camouflage shows the PECM antennas as dark panels on the side of the nose. There were more along the fuselage, in the wings and on the tail. By measuring the time an electronic signal took to arrive at the antennas, the angle could be determined to plot radar emitters. BuNo 151727 was stricken in Rota, Spain, in 1972.

8

RA-5C BuNo 151634/NK 125 of RVAH-12/CVW-14, USS *Constellation*, August 1967

On 13 August 1967, Lt Cdr Leo Hyatt and Lt(jg) Wayne Goodermote were on their 33rd mission together when BuNo 151634 was hit by AAA while doing 720 knots. Although the Vigilante was immediately enveloped in flame and the tail section soon came apart, both crewmen successfully ejected and were captured as soon as they touched down in their parachutes. They were eventually released in 1973.

9

RA-5C BuNo 149283/AA 606 of RVAH-11/CVW-17, USS *Forrestal*, 29 July 1967

As a supplement to West Coast aircraft carriers, Atlantic Fleet carriers would also go to *WestPac*. *Forrestal* with RVAH-11 on board, had been operating in the Tonkin Gulf for just five days when a disastrous fire broke out on the flight deck on 29 July 1967 and completely destroyed 21 aircraft from CVW-17, including RA-5Cs BuNos 148932, 149284 and 149305. Despite these losses, the squadron remained combat ready, and replacement aeroplanes were brought in and RVAH-11 returned to combat aboard *Kitty Hawk* in November of that same year. Undamaged BuNo 149283 operated with the unit from both CVA-60 and CVA-63 during 1967. Its checkerboard pattern on the tail harked back to VAH-11's days flying the A-3 'Whale'.

10

RA-5C BuNo 149297/NE 701 of RVAH-6/CVW-2, USS *Ranger*, early 1968

In comparison with the RVAH-6 jet seen in profile six, this aircraft is devoid of a nose slash and the number of *fleur-de-lis* on the tail stripe has risen by one to six. The commanding officer of RVAH-6, Cdr C C Smith, and Lt John Calhoun, made a significant discovery during a reconnaissance mission in this jet when their photographs revealed the exact location of the infamous 'Hanoi Hilton' prison camp in downtown Hanoi. The aeroplanes of RVAH-6 went from the heat of *Yankee Station* to the freezing cold of Korea in winter when the *Pueblo* was captured in January 1968. The maintenance facility at NAS Atsugi, in Japan, installed the first AAS-21 IR mapping equipment in 'Fleurs' RA-5Cs soon after CVA-61 headed back south to the Tonkin Gulf in mid March 1968.

11

RA-5C BuNo 149283/NH 606 of RVAH-11/CVW-11, USS *Kitty Hawk*, 18 May 1968

Also the subject of profile nine, BuNo 149283 retains the 'Checkertail' marking on its tail as worn when part of CVW-17, but its intake duct warning area has now been painted solid red. CVW-11's traditional NH tail code has also replaced CVW-17's AA. The executive officer of RVAH-11, Cdr Charlie James, and RAN, Lt Cdr Vincent Monroe, were flying 'Glen Rock 606' at 10,000 ft when the jet was hit by a large calibre AAA shell northwest of Vinh on 18 May 1968. Both men successfully ejected, but there was too much anti-aircraft fire in the area to attempt a rescue. James survived almost five years of imprisonment but Monroe did not.

12

RA-5C BuNo 149278/NG 102 of RVAH-1/CVW-9, USS *Enterprise*, May 1968

The small letter 'E' carried just forward of the 'Smokin' Tiger' emblem on this RA-5C denotes the winning of a Battle Efficiency award by RVAH-1. BuNo 149278, flying with the call-sign 'Comanche Trail 102', was on a photo run at 6500 ft near Ha Tinh on 5 May 1968 when, as the crew of its F-4 fighter escort described it, 'The "Vigi" burst into a huge fireball about twice the size of the aircraft and snap-rolled when the starboard wing came off'. Lts Giles Norrington and Dick Tangeman somehow managed to eject, but were injured in the process and quickly captured. Both men were released in March 1973.

13

RA-5C BuNo 149293/NK 113 of RVAH-5/CVW-14, USS *Constellation*, November 1968

Back for a second combat cruise after two trips to the Mediterranean, RVAH-5 had the IR AAS-21 mapper installed in its jets (the flat bulge on the bottom of the canoe with the rotating beacon light – when activated, a protective panel would slide open to expose the system's super-cooled sensing elements). 'Old Kentucky 113' (BuNo 149293) was the first Navy reconnaissance aircraft to be lost following the instigation of the 31 October 1968 bombing halt. On 25 November, radar-guided AAA tracked the wildly jinking RA-5C northwest of Vinh and eventually caused it to explode into four parts. Neither crew member survived.

14

RA-5C BuNo 150842/NG 604 of RVAH-6/CVW-9, USS *Enterprise*, 31 March 1969

BuNo 150842 was damaged during the *Enterprise* fire off of Hawaii on 14 January 1969. On the vessel's first day back on the line, on 31 March, Cdr Dan White, with RAN, Lt Ramey Carpenter, were flying northeast of Nakhon Phanom, in Laos, when 'Field Goal 604' (BuNo150842) burst into flames and fell apart. There were no ejections. RVAH-6 went north to Korea again on this deployment when a US Navy EC-121 surveillance aircraft was shot down in April 1969.

15

RA-5C BuNo 148928/NK 602 of RVAH-7/CVW-14, USS *Constellation*, 1 January 1970

Cdr Randell Billings, CO of CVW-14, borrowed BuNo 148928 while the air wing was ashore at NAS Cubi Point, in the Philippines, on New Year's Day 1970. His RAN for the flight was Lt(jg) Billy Beaver of RVAH-7. Something went wrong during the course of the sortie and the Vigilante went into a supersonic dive. When Lt(jg) Beaver could not get a response from the pilot he ejected. However, the RAN's neck was broken when he abandoned the jet at high speed and he was killed. CAG Billings went down with the aeroplane.

16

RA-5C BuNo 149307/NE 601 of RVAH-5/CVW-2, USS *Ranger*, 1970

Peering over the red arrow on the vertical tail of this machine a cryptic cartoon character known as the 'Mushmouth'. Associated with VC-, VAH- and RVAH-5, the 'Mushmouth' periodically decorated Savages, 'Whales' and Vigilantes between bouts of officious disapproval. The squadron's official call-sign was 'Old Kentucky' and legitimate nickname 'Savage Sons'.

17

RA-5C BuNo 156626/NH 604 of RVAH-6/CVW-11, USS *Kitty Hawk*, 1971

The names stencilled beneath the canopies of this Vigilante read *LCDR GASTROCK* and *LT CONRAD*, to which had been added *DYNAMIC DUO*, *CAPED CRUSADER* and *BOY WONDER*! On 22 April 1971, Gastrock and Conrad flew BuNo 156626 'Field Goal 604' on the *Blue Tree* mission to the airfield at Quan Lang. Under the rules of 'Protective Reaction', after the Vigilante was shot at, the strike aircraft of CVW-11 rolled in and destroyed two MiGs, gun sites and various support equipment. The wavy demarcation line and pale blue NAVY titling reveals that this aircraft was supplied to RVAH-6 straight from NAR just prior to the unit departing on cruise in early November 1970.

18

RA-5C BuNo 156622/NE 602 of RVAH-1/CVW-2, USS *Ranger*, 1970

Along with RVAH-6, the 'Smokin' Tigers' of RVAH-1 had the honour of taking the first newly-built '156 series' RA-5Cs to sea on their respective combat deployments, which commenced in the autumn of 1970. Externally, the new Vigilantes boasted an additional strake which ran from the wing leading edge to the top of the intake ducts. The engines were also upgraded to J79-GE-10s. Just 36 '156 series' jets were built for the Navy, and these allowed a number of older Vigilantes to be retired.

19

RA-5C BuNo 149276/AB 602 of RVAH-14/CVW-1, USS *John F Kennedy*, 1970

Known as the 'Eagle Eyes', RVAH-14 made three consecutive cruises on 'Big John' to the Mediterranean between 1969 and 1972, after which it completed its fourth, and last deployment, aboard *Independence* as part of CVW-7. On the latter cruise, the squadron was on the scene to monitor the Yom Kippur War, which erupted between Israel and its Arab neighbours in October 1973. BuNo 149276 was stricken at NAS Key West on 31 July 1976.

20

RA-5C BuNo 156634/NK 602 of RVAH-5/CVW-14, USS *Enterprise*, October 1971

On 17 October 1971, BuNo 156634 became the first RA-5C to be lost in *WestPac* since March 1969 when it flew into the water while on a routine training flight. The 'Savage Sons' commanding officer, Cdr L R 'Bud' Everett, and RAN, Lt Cdr Paul Stokes, were both killed.

21

RA-5C BuNo 149314/GJ 201 of RVAH-3, NAS Sanford, June 1967

RVAH-3 was called the 'Recce RAG' after it began training crews for the RA-5C. Its assigned Vigilantes went to sea only on Carrier Qualification detachments. RVAH-3 would have up to 14 RA-5Cs on strength, plus four TA-3s and four TA-4s, all of which had orange-striped tails. This aircraft was lost in a fatal crash (one crewman survived) on 14 June 1967 near the RAG's Sanford home.

22

RA-5C BuNo 156614/NG 604 of RVAH-11/CVW-9, USS *Constellation*, 1971/72

Some of RVAH-11's junior officers thought that the addition of shark's teeth to the intake warning triangles would be 'cool', and they convinced the CO to give it a try. However, due to the increased operational tempo in the lead up to the *Linebacker* campaign of May 1972, the idea was dropped after only this aeroplane was painted. BuNo 156614 later went to RVAH-6 on *Forrestal*, and was lost in the Mediterranean following an unsuccessful night catapult shot on 11 July 1974.

23

RA-5C BuNo 151618/NH 604 of RVAH-7/CVW-11, USS *Kitty Hawk*, May 1972

RVAH-7 carried out another major change to its tail markings prior to embarking on the marathon nine-month-long 1972 combat cruise in CVA-63. Crews names were carried in the black rectangles beneath the canopies, and the white E denoted the unit's attainment of that year's battle efficiency award. Squadron XO Cdr Ron Polfer and Lt(jg) Joe Kernan were shot down by AAA in BuNo 151618 near the infamous Thanh Hoa Bridge on 7 May 1972. After ejecting from a blazing 'Flare 04', both men were captured and released with the last group of PoWs the following year.

24

RA-5C BuNo 156616/AC 601 of RVAH-1/CVW-3, USS *Saratoga*, May 1972

Saratoga was another East Coast carrier which went to *WestPac* only once, while RVAH-1 was on its fourth trip there. Sailors in maintenance added nicknames to the normal *LCDR CHUCK SMITH* and *LT(JG) LARRY KUNZ* on the side of BuNo 156616. Smith became *SMILIN' JACK* and Kunz, *'BDT'*. Depending on who was asked, 'BDT' stood for 'Big Deadly Tiger' or 'Big Dumb Texan'. Smith and Kunz were hit by a SAM while flying in this

Vigilante on 7 June 1972. Ejecting over Haiphong Harbour, their helicopter rescue took 50 minutes, during which time both men came under constant fire from guns on the shore.

25

RA-5C BuNo 156623/AJ 603 of RVAH-6/CVW-8, USS *America*, December 1972

On 23 December 1972, BuNo 156623 (call-sign 'Fieldgoal 603') was on a weather alternate mission along the coastal islands off North Vietnam when its escort, F-4J BuNo 153885 ('Shamrock 210') of Marine squadron VMFA-333 was shot down by 85 mm AAA. The CO of RVAH-6, Cdr Jim Thompson, with his RAN, Lt Emy Conrad, stayed overhead the downed crew, drawing off the enemy gunners until SAR helicopters could extricate the Marines.

26

RA-5C BuNo 156633/NK 603 of RVAH-13/CVW-14, USS *Enterprise*, 28 December 1972

This aircraft was the last Vigilante to be lost during the Vietnam War, and the only one to be shot down in aerial combat. Lt Cdr Al Agnew, pilot, and Lt Mike Haifley, RAN, were on their second mission of the day in NK 603, heading east from Hanoi, when MiG threat warnings flooded the Guard frequency. Their F-4 escort advised them to break just as 'Atoll' missiles fired by a MiG-21 hit the Vigilante. Haifley was killed either in the initial missile impact or the crash which followed, but Agnew ejected and became a PoW.

27

RA-5C BuNo 156621/NE 614 of RVAH-5/CVW-2, USS *Ranger*, 28 December 1972

This aircraft featured crew names within red rectangles aft of the cockpit transparencies, these being the same colour as the arrow on the tail and the air wing code. BuNo 156621 survived the harried days of *Linebacker II* and is now on display on the flight deck of *Intrepid* in New York City.

28

RA-5C BuNo 149317/NG 601 of RVAH-12/CVW-9, USS *America*, 1970

Although an East Coast carrier, *America* made three combat deployments – once travelling completely around the world to reach the war zone, and the other two times halfway and back again. Its assigned air wing in 1970 was Pacific Fleet-based CVW-9.

29

RA-5C BuNo 156628/NK 601 of RVAH-12/CVW-14, USS *Enterprise*, 1975

Enterprise, with RVAH-12 embarked, was standing by during the evacuation and fall of Saigon in April 1975. With the end of hostilities, squadron paint schemes became brighter. Now down to three RA-5Cs per frontline unit, the 'Speartips' painted each nose differently – 601 had a red nose with a white band and blue stars, 602 had a blue nose with a white band and red stars and 603 had a white nose with a red band and white stars.

30

RA-5C BuNo 149299/GM 601 of RVAH-9, NAS Key West, 1976

All RVAH squadrons had a G-prefixed two-letter code for use when not assigned to an air wing. The 'Hooters' made a stylised owl out of their GM. BuNo 149299 was one of the original batch of RA-5Cs brought up to '156 series' standard when it went through overhaul. The aeroplane was finally stricken at NAS Key West on 20 September 1977.

COLOUR SECTION

1

An unidentified RA-5C with a camera silhouette and hash-marks indicating reconnaissance missions that it had flown. The windscreen exterior has been mended with a red plastic compound. The rail in the centre of the canopy was for the anti-blast light shield, although the shield itself was not installed (*EBAL*)

2

In this nose-on view, the effect of nosewheel steering on the vertical tail is apparent. The yaw augmentation system would be trying to adjust, and would cause the tail to shimmy (*Powell*)

3

An RVAH-1 RA-5C on *Independence* in 1965. The hardest part of getting on the catapult – getting the nosewheel over the shuttle and on the centreline – has been done. The holdback is slack behind the tail and the launch bridle over the shuttle is being held in place on the hooks under the engines. The signal the Cat Officer in the yellow shirt is giving is for the pilot to release his brakes, and for the catapult operator to take tension – apply enough steam pressure to keep the bridle and hold back taut. All personnel will clear away as the pilot goes to full power, and then into maximum afterburner, before signalling with a salute that he is ready to launch (*Woodul*)

4

Preparing an RVAH-1 Vigilante for a mission on *Independence* in 1965. The technician is working in the RAN's cockpit. The cable run from the deck into the panel behind the 'Smokin' Tiger' crest is providing the jet with electrical power so that its cockpit displays can be run up. The cable going into the nose is from the SINS (Ship's Inertial Navigation System), and it is updating the ASB-12's present position with great accuracy. The cables will not be removed until after the engines are started and the Vigilante is relying on its own power. Three fuel cans in 'train' sit on the deck behind the 'Vigis' (*Woodul*)

5
A brand new '156 series' prepares to be launched from CVA-63's waist cat one in 1970. RVAH-6 flew five aeroplanes with consecutive BuNos on this cruise – 156623 (shown here) to 156627. The cat officer at the right of the photo is giving the pilot his final launch signals. 'You drop your heels to the floor, but leave your toes on the rudders. Your left hand pushes the throttles to the detent for full military power. While the J79 engines spool-up, you look over to the catapult officer. He is waving his hand with two fingers up over his head. Eyes back in the cockpit to the engine gauges – RPM, temperatures, pressures are all good. The cat officer is flicking his hand from fist to fingers open to fist. Time for afterburner. Push the throttles past the detent as far forward as they go. Fast now, look at one tiny gauge with two needles – afterburner nozzle positions. They both swing around symmetrically. Too much time in burner will damage the sea water-cooled blast deflectors only feet behind the exhausts' (*Powell*)

6
This Vigilante, with NAA factory-applied wavy colour demarcation, was photographed on *Ranger* in 1964 during the RA-5C's first ever deployment. A flasher pod is mounted beneath the aircraft's right wing (*Wells*)

7
An overhead view of a '156 series' RA-5C in flight. Wing trailing edges were painted white as per the Navy policy of using this colour to adorn any flight control surfaces that faced a nuclear bomb blast left behind by the escaping aeroplane. On Vigilantes fresh from the NAA factory, the demarcation line on uppersurfaces was wavy – this was also the case along the fuselage sides. The stainless steel alloy leading edge droops were left unpainted because the hot bleed air would have charred the finish (*EBAL*)

8
An RVAH-14 'Vigi' moments after launch, before the pilot has raised the landing gear or the flaps. To mark its last deployment, RVAH-14 added a stylised eagle to the noses of its Vigilantes (*Harris*)

9
The CAG F-4J of VF-92 escorts an RVAH-11 Vigilante on a training flight during work-ups prior to the epic CVW-9 1971-72 cruise aboard *Constellation*. RA-5C BuNo 156614 later went to RVAH-6, and in July 1974, during a Mediterranean deployment on *Forrestal*, it suffered a catastrophic engine failure on a night catapult shot and crashed into the sea. Both crewmen were rescued (*EBAL*)

10
Two RVAH-6 jets formate for the camera during the unit's final cruise in 1978. The lead Vigilante is BuNo 156624, which wound up in the Pensacola museum in the markings shown here (*EBAL*)

11
A VA-65 KA-6D refuels an RVAH-5 Vigilante, while an F-4J from VF-96 waits its turn. RA-5C BuNo 156621 avoided the scrap yard and the bombing range to take its place on the flight deck of *Intrepid*, moored in New York City (*EBAL*)

12
Two A-7s and a KA-6 from the Patuxent River Test Center join up with an RVAH-9 RA-5C to conduct a fly-past overhead *Forrestal*. Following the demise of BuNo 156637 in a crash at Patuxent River in July 1973, the Test Center would borrow jets from fleet squadrons whenever the need arose (*EBAL*)

INDEX

References to illustrations are shown in **bold**.Colour Section illustrations are prefixed 'cs.', with page and caption locators in brackets.